EDITORS (

A Moment with GOD

Daily Scripture

Reflection

A Moment with God

Published by Guideposts Books & Inspirational Media, 100 Reserve Road, Suite E200,
Danbury, CT 06810
Guideposts.org

Acknowledgments

Every attempt has been made to credit the sources of copyrighted material used in this book. If any such acknowledgment has been inadvertently omitted or miscredited, receipt of such information would be appreciated.

Cover design by Serena Fox Design Company
Cover illustration by Dreamstime
Interior design by Serena Fox Design Company
Interior illustration by Dreamstime and Shutterstock
Typeset by Aptara, Inc.

ISBN 978-1-959633-80-8 (hardcover)
ISBN 978-1-961125-72-8 (softcover)
ISBN 978-1-959633-88-4 (epub)

Printed and bound in the United States of America

What lies behind you and what lies in front of you,
pales in comparison to what lies inside of you.

—Ralph Waldo Emerson

Day 1

Therefore, if anyone is in Christ, the new creation has come: The old has gone, the new is here!

2 Corinthians 5:17 (NIV)

Reflect

We will open the book. Its pages are blank. We are going to put words on them ourselves. The book is called Opportunity and its first chapter begins today.

Edith Lovejoy Pierce, poet

Act

Start today committed to a new life.

Pray

Heavenly Father, because of Your strength, I can let go of the past and step forward with faith.

Day 2

Be thankful in all circumstances, for this is God's will for you who belong to Christ Jesus.

1 Thessalonians 5:18 (NLT)

Reflect

"Thank you" is the best prayer that anyone could say. I say that one a lot. "Thank you" expresses extreme gratitude, humility, understanding.

Alice Walker

Act

When facing a situation that seems confusing or upsetting, thank God for His understanding.

Pray

Heavenly Father, I can endure any situation because I know You are working on my behalf. I'm safe in Your hands.

Day 3

In peace I will lie down and sleep, for you alone, Lord, make me dwell in safety.

Psalm 4:8 (NIV)

Reflect

A well-spent day brings happy sleep.

Leonardo da Vinci

Act

Before you go to sleep, commit your soul to God's care.

Pray

Heavenly Father, fortify me each night with Your peace. Watch over me; bless my house and my loved ones. Help me rest in Your promise.

Day 4

Every word of God is flawless; he is a shield to those who take refuge in him.

Proverbs 30:5 (NIV)

Reflect

The Bible is the only book whose Author is always present when one reads it.

Author Unknown

Act

Allow God's love to heal old wounds.

Pray

Heavenly Father, replace my pain with Your love.

Day 5

Brothers, I do not consider that I have made it my own. But one thing I do: forgetting what lies behind and straining forward to what lies ahead, I press on toward the goal for the prize of the upward call of God in Christ Jesus.

Philippians 3:13–14 (ESV)

Reflect

Problems are to the mind what exercise is to the muscles, they toughen and make strong.

Norman Vincent Peale, pastor and author

Act

Think of five events or choices that seemed like detours at the time, then thank Jesus for using those detours to get you someplace better.

Pray

Heavenly Father, open my heart and clear my vision so that I may follow Your path.

Day 6

Let all the people of Jerusalem shout his praise with joy! For great is the Holy One of Israel who lives among you.

Isaiah 12:6 (NLT)

Reflect

Trials...may come in abundance. But they cannot penetrate into the sanctuary of the soul when it is settled in God, and we may dwell in perfect peace.

Hannah Whitall Smith, author

Act

Believe that God will bring you through hardship—true joy is always in reach.

Pray

Lord, thank You for showing me that in the midst of trials and difficulties, I can be joyful because You are in my life.

Day 7

If I should count them, they would be more in number than the sand; when I awake, I am still with You.

Psalm 139:18 (NKJV)

Reflect

This a wonderful day. I've never seen this one before.

Maya Angelou, author and poet

Act

Keep this Scripture close to your heart. It is the secret to having a wonderful day, every day.

Pray

Heavenly Father, open my eyes to the blessings of today. Wake me up with excitement and hope for the dawning of a new day.

Day 8

**The LORD is my strength and my defense;
he has become my salvation.**

Psalm 118:14 (NIV)

Reflect

God enters by a private door into each individual.

Ralph Waldo Emerson, philosopher and poet

Act

Cultivate the conviction that you are not alone,
that God is with you.

Pray

Lord, You have redeemed me and claimed me and
given me a strength that is not my own.

Day 9

Call to me and I will answer you and tell you great and unsearchable things you do not know.

Jeremiah 33:3 (NIV)

Reflect

Weave in faith and God will find the thread.

Proverb

Act

Believe in the sun even when it's not shining.

Pray

Lord, teach me to trust You to lead me down a path through the darkness.

Day 10

He will respond to the prayer of the destitute; he will not despise their plea.

Psalm 102:17 (NIV)

Reflect

A chief cause of worry and unhappiness in life is trading what we want most for what we want at the moment.

Maralee McKee, author

Act

Pray and release your worries.

Pray

Dear Lord, help me to remember Your peace is in my reach, no matter what circumstances I face.

Day 11

**Because your love is better than life,
my lips will glorify you.**

Psalm 63:3 (NIV)

Reflect

The safest place to be is within the will of God.

Author Unknown

Act

Face your challenges with determination
and resiliency.

Pray

Lord, help us to trust You as we walk through
our lives.

Day 12

Haven't you yet learned that your body is the home of the Holy Spirit God gave you, and that he lives within you? Your own body does not belong to you.

1 Corinthians 6:19 (TLB)

Reflect

We fail in the work of grace and love when there is too much of us and not enough of God.

Suzanne Woods Fisher, author

Act

Be patient, have faith, and work toward what you desire.

Pray

Lord, thank You for the grace that strengthens me for tasks large and small.

Day 13

Now faith is confidence in what we hope for and assurance about what we do not see.

Hebrews 11:1 (NIV)

Reflect

Faith is taking the first step even when you don't see the whole staircase.

Martin Luther King, Jr.

Act

Believe in God's power to transform you and situations around you.

Pray

Dear Lord, guide me toward Your plan. Help me to take the first step.

Day 14

Jesus replied, "What is impossible with man is possible with God."

Luke 18:27 (NIV)

Reflect

At least at times of loss, we are reminded of our priorities, of our many blessings. In times of gain, we can so often lose our way.

Mindy Starns Clark, author

Act

Take comfort knowing God is with you.

Pray

Heavenly Father, we thank You for the comfort you give us when we come to You.

Day 15

Fight the good fight of the faith. Take hold of the eternal life to which you were called when you made your good confession in the presence of many witnesses.

1 Timothy 6:12 (NIV)

Reflect

Our prayers run along one road and God's answers by another, and by and by they meet.

Adoniram Judson, missionary

Act

Practice believing that as you pray, you are receiving God's boundless blessings.

Pray

Father, keep me from trying to do it all, that I might rest and walk in Your grace.

Day 16

...a time to weep and a time to laugh, a time to mourn and a time to dance...

Ecclesiastes 3:4 (NIV)

Reflect

The most wasted of all days is one without laughter.

E. E. Cummings, poet

Act

Awaken the laughter in your heart.

Pray

Dear Lord, remind me that it's how I live that reveals who I really am.

Day 17

Commit your way to the Lord; trust in him and he will do this: He will make your righteous reward shine like the dawn, your vindication like the noonday sun.

Psalm 37:5–6 (NIV)

Reflect

Faith is not the belief that God will do what you want. It is the belief that God will do what is right.

Max Lucado, pastor and author

Act

Believe that Jesus Christ is with you, helping you now, and that through Him your life can be changed.

Pray

Lord, all things are possible if we believe. Thank You for loving us enough to send what we need.

Day 18

Glorify the LORD with me; let us exalt his name together.

Psalm 34:3 (NIV)

Reflect

Let gratitude be the pillow upon which you kneel to say your nightly prayer. And let faith be the bridge you build to overcome evil and welcome good.

Maya Angelou, author and poet

Act

Approach today with a grateful heart.

Pray

Heavenly Father, grant me the courage to serve You faithfully in every person I meet.

Day 19

...for God's gifts and his call are irrevocable.

Romans 11:29 (NIV)

Reflect

Worship is a way of gladly reflecting back to God the radiance of His worth.

John Piper, pastor, theologian, and author

Act

Remember that remarkable achievements begin as thoughts.

Pray

Lord, the greatest success I can achieve is to know You and love You and to help others know and love You too.

Day 20

Let the heavens rejoice, let the earth be glad; let them say among the nations, "The LORD reigns!"

1 Chronicles 16:31 (NIV)

Reflect

Great opportunities to help others seldom come, but small ones surround us every day.

Sally Koch, author

Act

Blossom into the best that you can be.

Pray

Dear God, may I do my part to love and change the world.

Day 21

And whatever you do, whether in word or deed, do it all in the name of the Lord Jesus, giving thanks to God the Father through him.

Colossians 3:17 (NIV)

Reflect

Good morning, Lord! What are You up to today? Can I be a part of it? Thank You. Amen.

Norman Grubb, missionary, writer, and teacher

Act

Concentrate on now and your dreams will become your future.

Pray

Father, in every moment of every day, a choice waits. Help me to always choose the good.

Day 22

Consider it pure joy, my brothers and sisters, whenever you face trials of many kinds, because you know that the testing of your faith produces perseverance. Let perseverance finish its work so that you may be mature and complete, not lacking anything.

James 1:2–4 (NIV)

Reflect

To know God's will, say, "I will" to God.

Author Unknown

Act

Ask God to open your eyes to the unexpected ways He is working.

Pray

Heavenly Father, please help me face each day with grace and appreciation for the blessings of Your love.

Day 23

The Lord replied, "My Presence will go with you, and I will give you rest."

Exodus 33:14 (NIV)

Reflect

Few delights can equal the mere presence of one whom we trust utterly.

George MacDonald, minister, author, and poet

Act

Trust that there is a divine plan.

Pray

Lord, thank You for renewing me and giving me a life that has purpose and meaning.

Day 24

And hope does not put us to shame, because God's love has been poured out into our hearts through the Holy Spirit, who has been given to us.

Romans 5:5 (NIV)

Reflect

Open your hearts to the love God instills...God loves you tenderly. What He gives you is not to be kept under lock and key, but to be shared.

Mother Teresa

Act

This month, look at your schedule and find opportunities to do something in service of God.

Pray

God, remind me to share with others what You have been doing in my life.

Day 25

Your eyes saw my unformed body; all the days ordained for me were written in your book before one of them came to be.

Psalm 139:16 (NIV)

Reflect

Faith is the strength by which a shattered world shall emerge into the light.

Helen Keller

Act

Always be ready to learn and grow.

Pray

Lord, light my way along Your path so that all I do leads me toward the destination You have in mind.

Day 26

The thief comes only to steal and kill and destroy; I have come that they may have life, and have it to the full.

John 10:10 (NIV)

Reflect

It is such comfort to drop the tangles of life into God's hands and leave them there.

Anonymous

Act

Put God first in your life.

Pray

Dear Lord, help me to remember that I can always depend on You.

Day 27

For God is not a God of disorder but of peace—as in all the congregations of the Lord's people.

1 Corinthians 14:33 (NIV)

Reflect

Worry is a thin stream of fear that trickles through the mind, which, if encouraged, will cut a channel so wide that all other thoughts will be drained out.

Author Unknown

Act

Learn to think calmly and confidently, no matter what comes your way.

Pray

Dear Lord, help me to remember that Your peace is in my reach, no matter what circumstances I face.

Day 28

But if any of you lacks wisdom, let him ask of God, who gives to all generously and without reproach, and it will be given to him.

James 1:5 (NASB)

Reflect

Isn't it nice to think that tomorrow is a new day with no mistakes in it yet?

L. M. Montgomery, author

Act

Look for an opportunity to make a positive difference.

Pray

Heavenly Father, keep my spirit open today to the power of Your guidance and strength.

Day 29

**Oh give thanks to the Lord, for he is good,
for his steadfast love endures forever!**

Psalm 107:1 (ESV)

Reflect

Love is the only thing that we can carry with us when we go, and it makes the end so easy.

Louisa May Alcott, writer

Act

Open your heart to God's amazing love.

Pray

Heavenly Father, how great and steadfast is Your love! Help me recognize the mercies and blessings You bestow upon me today and every day.

Day 30

Though you have not seen him, you love him. Though you do not now see him, you believe in him and rejoice with joy that is inexpressible and filled with glory.

1 Peter 1:8 (ESV)

Reflect

Find out where joy resides and give it a voice far beyond singing. For to miss the joy is to miss all.

Robert Louis Stevenson, writer

Act

Give everything to God, and He will give you everything too!

Pray

Lord, help me to understand that I can be joyful at all times and in all situations, because I am Your child and You are my God.

Day 31

Do everything in love.

1 Corinthians 16:14 (NIV)

Reflect

Faith is about doing. You are how you act, not just how you believe.

Mitch Albom, author

Act

If you catch yourself wishing or hoping for something, stop and lift your eyes to heaven and turn those thoughts into a prayer.

Pray

Lord, day by day, help me to do what You have designed me to do.

Day 32

You, Lord, are forgiving and good, abounding in love to all who call to you.

Psalm 86:5 (NIV)

Reflect

Sometimes God makes better choices for us than we could have ever made for ourselves.

Jennifer Hudson Taylor, author

Act

Ask Jesus to remind you that a kind deed is never wrong.

Pray

Father, of all the gifts and blessings You bestow on us, the greatest is the miracle of life. Let me find joy and satisfaction in every amazing, improbable moment.

Day 33

Remind the people to be subject to rulers and authorities, to be obedient, to be ready to do whatever is good, to slander no one, to be peaceable and considerate, and always to be gentle toward everyone.

Titus 3:1–2 (NIV)

Reflect

Your prayer for someone may or may not change them, but it always changes you.

Craig Groeschel, pastor

Act

Concentrate on helping others, and grasp every opportunity to offer encouragement.

Pray

Father, may my prayers for others be as constant and natural as breathing.

Day 34

But the Lord said to Samuel, "Do not consider his appearance or his height, for I have rejected him. The Lord does not look at the things people look at. People look at the outward appearance, but the Lord looks at the heart."

1 Samuel 16:7 (NIV)

Reflect

At the end of your time here, the world will either be more or less kind, compassionate, generous, funny, creative, and loving because of your presence in it—and you alone get to choose.

John Pavlovitz, pastor

Act

Use your words to uplift yourself and others.

Pray

You fill me with concern for others, Lord, and You give me strength to help them.

Day 35

Help us, God our Savior, for the glory of your name; deliver us and forgive our sins for your name's sake.

Psalm 79:9 (NIV)

Reflect

Never forget the three powerful resources you always have available to you: love, prayer, and forgiveness.

H. Jackson Brown, Jr., author

Act

Pray about what you want. Ask God if it is the right thing for you.

Pray

Dear Lord, one of Your most precious gifts is forgiveness. How I thank You for that!

Day 36

I thank God, whom I serve, as my ancestors did, with a clear conscience, as night and day I constantly remember you in my prayers.

2 Timothy 1:3 (NIV)

Reflect

Our greatest comfort in sorrow is to know that God is in control.

Lynn Thornton, writer

Act

Cast your cares on the Lord, for He cares.

Pray

Dear God, hold our hands as we journey onward.

Day 37

Cast your burden on the LORD, And He shall sustain you; He shall never permit the righteous to be moved.

Psalm 55:22 (NKJV)

Reflect

Faith means being sure of what we hope for now. It means knowing something is real, this moment, all around you, even when you don't see it.

Joni Eareckson Tada, author

Act

Make a commitment to read a psalm or proverb every day to help you absorb divine words that will change your life.

Pray

Lord, help me hear Your call and serve You joyfully.

Day 38

To everything there is a season, a time for every purpose under heaven.

Ecclesiastes 3:1 (NKJV)

Reflect

Put your trust in God and just calmly go your way.

Norman Vincent Peale, pastor and author

Act

Recognize that your faith will lead you to great things.

Pray

Thank You, Jesus, for the precious moments when You bless my worship with Your Holy Spirit.

Day 39

For no word from God will ever fail.

Luke 1:37 (NIV)

Reflect

God never made a promise that was
too good to be true.

Dwight L. Moody, evangelist and publisher

Act

Lean on the One who cares.

Pray

Lord, help me to believe and act on Your promise.

Day 40

Do not merely listen to the word, and so deceive yourselves. Do what it says.

James 1:22 (NIV)

Reflect

Love is the story and the prayer that matters the most.

Brian Doyle, author

Act

Be willing to take lovingly each small gift of life.

Pray

God, thank You for the moments that wake me up to this perfectly beautiful world.

Day 41

Wealth and honor come from you; you are the ruler of all things. In your hands are strength and power to exalt and give strength to all.

1 Chronicles 29:12 (NIV)

Reflect

The only difference between stumbling blocks and stepping stones is the way in which we use them.

Anonymous

Act

When you feel fearful or troubled, ask Jesus to whisper reassurance to your spirit.

Pray

God, just for one day, let me see only the good. Give me the eyes of faith and the heart of hope.

Day 42

Make every effort to live in peace with everyone and to be holy; without holiness no one will see the Lord.

Hebrews 12:14 (NIV)

Reflect

There is no place so awake and alive as becoming.

Sue Monk Kidd, author

Act

Ask God to give you the grace to know Him more.

Pray

Lord, I pray that I grow closer and closer to You every day.

Day 43

And receive from him anything we ask, because we keep his commands and do what pleases him.

1 John 3:22 (NIV)

Reflect

The greatest achievements were at first and for a time dreams. The oak sleeps in the acorn.

James Allen, author

Act

Put aside your fear of failure and replace it with effort toward your goals.

Pray

Lord, help me keep my eyes on You and not on my fears.

Day 44

But blessed is the one who trusts in the LORD, whose confidence is in him.

Jeremiah 17:7 (NIV)

Reflect

If you have a song of faith in your heart, it will be heard by the look on your face.

Anonymous

Act

Approach the day with a joyful attitude.

Pray

Dear Lord, help me to open myself up to the happiness that is mine today.

Day 45

For it is by grace you have been saved, through faith—and this is not from yourselves, it is the gift of God—not by works, so that no one can boast.

Ephesians 2:8–9 (NIV)

Reflect

You will find it is necessary to let things go, simply for the reason that they are too heavy.

Corrie ten Boom, writer

Act

Replace your restlessness with patience, contentment, and peace.

Pray

Lord, keep me faithful in serving You all the days of my life.

Day 46

But our God formed the earth by his power and wisdom, and by his intelligence he hung the stars in space and stretched out the heavens.

Jeremiah 10:12 (TLB)

Reflect

Prayer is the exercise of drawing on the grace of God.

Oswald Chambers, author and evangelist

Act

Become more aware of the blessings that surround you.

Pray

Thank You, Jesus, for the extraordinary ways You work in my life.

Day 47

Your eyes will see the king in his beauty and view a land that stretches afar.

Isaiah 33:17 (NIV)

Reflect

Don't let the noise of the world keep you from hearing the voice of God.

Author Unknown

Act

Concentrate on serving God in whatever way He directs.

Pray

Lord, may all that I do be praise for Your glory.

Day 48

The Lord your God is with you, the Mighty Warrior who saves. He will take great delight in you; in his love he will no longer rebuke you, but will rejoice over you with singing.

Zephaniah 3:17 (NIV)

Reflect

In those times I can't seem to find God, I rest in the assurance that He knows how to find me.

Neva Coyle, writer

Act

Ask Jesus to be your GPS and practice surrendering your plans to Him.

Pray

Lord, in all the times and places of my life, Your love never leaves me.

Day 49

But be sure to fear the LORD and serve him faithfully with all your heart; consider what great things he has done for you.

1 Samuel 12:24 (NIV)

Reflect

We need never shout across the spaces to an absent God. He is nearer than our own soul, closer than our most secret thought.

A. W. Tozer, pastor and author

Act

Express your gratitude for something good that has come your way.

Pray

Lord, thank You for the delights of family and home. Show me how to use my time wisely so I may fully enjoy them.

Day 50

So God created human beings in his own image. In the image of God he created them; male and female he created them.

Genesis 1:27 (NLT)

Reflect

Jesus tends to His people individually. He personally sees to our needs. We all receive Jesus's touch. We experience His care.

Max Lucado, pastor and author

Act

Take an action today, such as watching the sunrise, to remember Jesus's great love for you.

Pray

Dear Lord, thank You for surrounding me with Your perfect love.

Day 51

Give thanks to the LORD, for he is good; his love endures forever.

Psalm 118:29 (NIV)

Reflect

Four things let us ever keep in mind: God hears prayer, God heeds prayer, God answers prayer, and God delivers by prayer.

E. M. Bounds, author

Act

Believe God loves you and is present in every aspect of your life.

Pray

Lord, show me new ways to bring comfort and healing in Your name.

Day 52

So do not fear, for I am with you; do not be dismayed, for I am your God. I will strengthen you and help you; I will uphold you with my righteous right hand.

Isaiah 41:10 (NIV)

Reflect

Wherever you are, be all there. Live to the hilt every situation you believe to be the will of God.

Jim Elliot

Act

Confidently trust God to handle things beyond your efforts.

Pray

Heavenly Father, You are miraculously working in each of us. Because of You, nothing is impossible!

Day 53

With joy you will draw water from the wells of salvation.

Isaiah 12:3 (NIV)

Reflect

Begin each day renewed, refreshed, and glad to be alive.

Norman Vincent Peale, pastor and author

Act

Ask Jesus to remove anything that is keeping you from growing in Him.

Pray

Lord, thank You for giving us the ability to learn, grow, and refresh ourselves in new and different ways.

Day 54

Arise, shine, for your light has come, and the glory of the Lord rises upon you.

Isaiah 60:1 (NIV)

Reflect

Take my moments and my days, let them flow in ceaseless prayer.

Frances Havergal, poet and hymn writer

Act

Use today as an opportunity to listen to God's voice.

Pray

Keep me aware today, Father, that I am walking in Your light.

Day 55

Who is going to harm you if you are eager to do good? But even if you should suffer for what is right, you are blessed. "Do not fear their threats; do not be frightened."

1 Peter 3:13–14 (NIV)

Reflect

Faith expects from God what is beyond all expectation.

Andrew Murray, writer and pastor

Act

Continue to expand your goals.

Pray

Creator God, You have given me life. May I use it to bless others.

Day 56

The generous will prosper; those who refresh others will themselves be refreshed.

Proverbs 11:25 (NLT)

Reflect

God shapes the world by prayer. The more prayer there is in the world, the better the world will be.

E. M. Bounds, author

Act

Be the subtle voice that helps another in need.

Pray

Dear Lord, help me to remember that the brightness of Your loving presence is always with me.

Day 57

Be joyful in hope, patient in affliction, faithful in prayer.

Romans 12:12 (NIV)

Reflect

Unwrap the hidden beauties in an ordinary day.

Gerhard E. Frost, author

Act

Find joy where and when it surfaces.

Pray

Lord, as hard as it is, help us to find joy in the difficult things that come our way, because we know You have given us the ultimate victory.

Day 58

Therefore, rid yourselves of all malice and all deceit, hypocrisy, envy, and slander of every kind.

1 Peter 2:1 (NIV)

Reflect

Of all the liars in the world, sometimes the worst are your own fears.

Rudyard Kipling, writer

Act

Ask Jesus to help you trust Him and to remind you that He is always enough.

Pray

Lord, You know my fears. Please give me the courage to do what I fear I can't.

Day 59

Rejoice always.

1 Thessalonians 5:16 (NIV)

Reflect

A quiet morning with a loving God puts the events of the upcoming day into proper perspective.

Janette Oke, author

Act

Pray about what you want. Ask God if it is the right thing for you.

Pray

Father, I praise You for providing moments of illumination that encourage me in my walk.

Day 60

You need to persevere so that when you have done the will of God, you will receive what he has promised.

Hebrews 10:36 (NIV)

Reflect

Sometimes your only available transportation is a leap of faith.

Margaret Shepard, author

Act

Do your best and leave the rest to God.

Pray

Heavenly Father, You have given me life. May I use it to bless others.

Day 61

Is anyone among you in trouble? Let them pray. Is anyone happy? Let them sing songs of praise.

James 5:13 (NIV)

Reflect

Faith comes through God's Word and through praise. Faith grows as you praise the Lord.

Wesley L. Duewel, author

Act

Walk through each room in your home and ask Jesus to help you find your shelter in Him.

Pray

God, I submit the struggles in my life to Your care.

Day 62

**The one who gets wisdom loves life;
the one who cherishes understanding
will soon prosper.**

Proverbs 19:8 (NIV)

Reflect

The Christian life is not a constant high. I have my moments of deep discouragement. I have to go to God in prayer with tears in my eyes and say, O God, forgive me, or help me.

Billy Graham

Act

Don't lose perspective when dealing with problems.

Pray

Lord, help me to find renewal from my difficulties by remembering that nothing happens out of Your control.

Day 63

It is God who arms me with strength and keeps my way secure.

2 Samuel 22:33 (NIV)

Reflect

Sometimes, all it takes is just one prayer to change everything.

Anonymous

Act

Tell Jesus what you're afraid of, then step out and live unafraid.

Pray

Help me to trust You in all things, Lord, and to leave the results to You.

Day 64

For now we see only a reflection as in a mirror; then we shall see face to face. Now I know in part; then I shall know fully, even as I am fully known.

1 Corinthians 13:12 (NIV)

Reflect

We are all wounded. But wounds are necessary for God's healing light to enter into our beings. Without wounds and failures and frustrations and defeats, there will be no opening for His brilliance to trickle in and invade our lives.

Bo Sanchez, author

Act

Realize you are greater than you ever considered yourself to be.

Pray

Lord, help me always to be open to Your calling.

Day 65

Ask and it will be given to you; seek and you will find; knock and the door will be opened to you.

Matthew 7:7 (NIV)

Reflect

Too many of us are not living our dreams because we are living our fears.

Les Brown, motivational speaker

Act

Turn your dream into a goal and focus on how to achieve it.

Pray

Lord, let me be guided by Your instructions.

Day 66

To You, God of my fathers, I give thanks and praise, for You have given me wisdom and power.

Daniel 2:23 (NASB)

Reflect

When a person doesn't have gratitude, something is missing in his or her humanity.

Elie Wiesel, writer

Act

Take a walk or hike and thank Jesus for how He guides you away from dangers in your journey through life.

Pray

Dear Lord, thank You for giving us a fresh start each day to begin anew.

Day 67

But I tell you, love your enemies and pray for those who persecute you.

Matthew 5:44 (NIV)

Reflect

Love is when the other person's happiness is more important than your own.

H. Jackson Brown

Act

Never dwell on bitterness, anger, or despair.

Pray

Lord, help us to appreciate and accept each other for the unique persons You created us to be.

Day 68

Evening, morning and noon I cry out in distress, and he hears my voice.

Psalm 55:17 (NIV)

Reflect

In times of hardship, you have to stop asking God, Why? and ask, What next?

Anonymous

Act

Take charge of your thoughts instead of letting them control you.

Pray

Help me wait patiently for Your answer, Lord.

Day 69

Therefore encourage one another and build each other up, just as in fact you are doing.

1 Thessalonians 5:11 (NIV)

Reflect

God has given us two hands—one to receive with and the other to give with. We are not cisterns made for hoarding; we are channels made for sharing.

Billy Graham

Act

Open your heart to the kindness of others.

Pray

Lord, I am in awe of the human spirit that grows stronger and more beautiful with life's challenges.

Day 70

I lie down and sleep; I wake again, because the Lord sustains me.

Psalm 3:5 (NIV)

Reflect

Go out on a limb when you pray for others. Take a risk. Be outrageous. Be passionate. Take a leap. Love a lot, not just a little.

Rick Hamlin, author

Act

Share with others how important they are to you.

Pray

Spirit of Love, I ask to wake each day of this year with fresh eyes, that I may see Your light shining through all my loved ones.

Day 71

He is the Rock, his works are perfect, and all his ways are just. A faithful God who does no wrong, upright and just is he.

Deuteronomy 32:4 (NIV)

Reflect

Pray, hope, don't worry.

Saint Padre Pio

Act

Hold onto God's promises—they will protect you from fear and lead you to joy.

Pray

Dear Lord, help me to begin today with hope, to feel Your love and know I am never alone.

Day 72

Give to the one who asks you, and do not turn away from the one who wants to borrow from you.

Matthew 5:42

Reflect

The world is full of angels; if you can't find one, be one.

Matshona Dhliwayo

Act

Fill your heart with strength and love for each other.

Pray

You fill me with concern for others, Lord, and You give me strength to help them.

Day 73

Set your minds on things above, not on earthly things.

Colossians 3:2 (NIV)

Reflect

Life's challenges are not supposed to paralyze you, they are supposed to help you discover who you are.

Bernice Johnson Reagon, composer

Act

When fear comes, counter it with an affirmation of faith.

Pray

Lord, in a world filled with change and uncertainty You are my constant Hope.

Day 74

In everything I did, I showed you that by this kind of hard work we must help the weak, remembering the words the Lord Jesus himself said: "It is more blessed to give than to receive."

Acts 20:35 (NIV)

Reflect

Have a sincere desire to serve God and mankind, and stop doubting, stop thinking negatively. Simply start living by faith, pray earnestly and humbly, and get into the habit of looking expectantly for the best.

Norman Vincent Peale, pastor and author

Act

Don't let your doubts blind you from your goals.

Pray

Nothing is too hard for me, Lord, as long as it takes me back to You.

Day 75

LORD my God, I called to you for help, and you healed me.

Psalm 30:2 (NIV)

Reflect

Darkness cannot drive out darkness; only light can do that. Hate cannot drive out hate; only love can do that.

Martin Luther King, Jr.

Act

Confidently trust God to handle things beyond your efforts.

Pray

Lord, help me to bring the dark places of my life into the sunlight of Your promise.

Day 76

Come, let us bow down in worship, let us kneel before the Lord our Maker.

Psalm 95:6 (NIV)

Reflect

Love wholeheartedly, be surprised, give thanks and praise—then you will discover the fullness of your life.

Brother David Steindl-Rast, author, scholar, and Benedictine monk

Act

Every day, affirm that you can make something really good out of your life.

Pray

Heavenly Father, keep my spirit open today to the power of Your guidance and strength.

Day 77

So we say with confidence, "The Lord is my helper; I will not be afraid. What can mere mortals do to me?"

Hebrews 13:6 (NIV)

Reflect

No pessimist ever discovered the secrets of the stars, or sailed to an uncharted land, or opened a new heaven to the human spirit.

Helen Keller

Act

Look at the stars at night and meditate on the mystery that the same God who set the stars in the sky lives in you.

Pray

Dear Lord, help me to remember that the brightness of Your loving presence is always with me.

Day 78

Like apples of gold in settings of silver is a ruling rightly given. Like an earring of gold or an ornament of fine gold is the rebuke of a wise judge to a listening ear.

Proverbs 25:11–12 (NIV)

Reflect

Kind words can be short and easy to speak, but their echoes are truly endless.

Mother Teresa

Act

Make someone's day. Tell them how much you appreciate them.

Pray

Dear Lord, help me to remember that my words hold power. Help me use them only to heal, help, and encourage another.

Day 79

A good man brings good things out of the good stored up in his heart, and an evil man brings evil things out of the evil stored up in his heart. For the mouth speaks what the heart is full of.

Luke 6:45 (NIV)

Reflect

To be grateful is to recognize the love of God in everything He has given us—and He has given us everything.

Thomas Merton, writer and poet

Act

Make a list of ten people or events that have blessed your life. Watch your heart bubble over in a spirit of gratitude and praise toward Jesus.

Pray

Thank You, Lord, for the people who stand with me at all times.

Day 80

In their hearts humans plan their course, but the LORD establishes their steps.

Proverbs 16:9 (NIV)

Reflect

We may live victoriously, not because we have any power within ourselves, but because when we give ourselves to God, He gives himself to us.

Norman Vincent Peale, pastor and author

Act

Be open to God's plan and will.

Pray

Lord, I am so thankful You're with me throughout the day. Let me see every morning as a fresh start.

Day 81

Jesus answered, "I am the way and the truth and the life. No one comes to the Father except through me."

John 14:6 (NIV)

Reflect

In the silence we listen to ourselves. Then we ask questions of ourselves. We describe ourselves, and in the quietude we may even hear the voice of God.

Maya Angelou, author and poet

Act

Think of your day as a channel for God's blessings.

Pray

Dear Lord, help me keep close to You today. Whatever strength I possess comes from You.

Day 82

He saved us, not because of righteous things we had done, but because of his mercy. He saved us through the washing of rebirth and renewal by the Holy Spirit.

Titus 3:5 (NIV)

Reflect

Courage is born at the point where God's grace and human effort intersect.

Father Timothy M. Gallagher, author

Act

Live with the thought of being in God's care.

Pray

Lord, give me the courage to stretch past my safe boundaries.

Day 83

The Lord is my strength and my defense; he has become my salvation. He is my God, and I will praise him, my father's God, and I will exalt him.

Exodus 15:2 (NIV)

Reflect

What God brings you to, God takes you through.

Sharon Connors, pastor and author

Act

Take comfort knowing God is with you.

Pray

Dear Lord, help me to persevere in prayer when things seem impossible, knowing that You are the God of possibilities.

Day 84

And without faith it is impossible to please God, because anyone who comes to him must believe that he exists and that he rewards those who earnestly seek him.

Hebrews 11:6 (NIV)

Reflect

One of the best ways to demonstrate God's love is to listen to people.

Bruce Larsen, author

Act

Today, listen more than you speak.

Pray

Dear Lord, may I give to someone today my friendship. May I let them rest in my love and care.

Day 85

Therefore I tell you, whatever you ask for in prayer, believe that you have received it, and it will be yours.

Mark 11:24 (NIV)

Reflect

If we don't change, we don't grow.
If we don't grow, we aren't really living.

Gail Sheehy, author

Act

Write down and commit to Jesus three areas in which you'd like to grow. Ask Him to make them new.

Pray

Lord, hold onto me as I go forward with faith in You.

Day 86

I thank Christ Jesus our Lord, who has given me strength, that he considered me trustworthy, appointing me to his service.

1 Timothy 1:12 (NIV)

Reflect

Upon a life I did not live, upon a death I did not die, I risk my whole eternity on the resurrection.

Charles H. Spurgeon, preacher

Act

Spend time with God, thanking Him for all He has done for you.

Pray

You are the Author of life, Lord; write Your renewing love upon my heart.

Day 87

And as they were coming down the mountain, he charged them to tell no one what they had seen, until the Son of Man had risen from the dead.

Mark 9:9 (ESV)

Reflect

Now Jesus Christ says that there is nothing in this world—sin, hate, frustration, pain, sorrow, evil, or death itself—that can defeat you if you are in Him, for He is the resurrection and the life. And so are you, if you are in Him.

Norman Vincent Peale, pastor and author

Act

Fill your heart with the glory of the Resurrection.

Pray

Risen Lord, help me to remember the difference Your Resurrection makes, today and every day.

Day 88

The righteous cry out, and the Lord hears them; he delivers them from all their troubles.

Psalm 34:17 (NIV)

Reflect

The opposite of joy is not sorrow. It is unbelief.

Leslie Weatherhead, Christian theologian

Act

Relax and accept God's grace in times of stress.

Pray

Father, thank You for the opportunities of renewal You grant me each and every day.

Day 89

Do not be like them, for your Father knows what you need before you ask him.

Matthew 6:8 (NIV)

Reflect

Faith will lead you where you cannot walk. Reason has never been a mountain climber.

E. W. Kenyon, pastor

Act

Face every situation with faith in your heart.

Pray

Lord God, help me carry the blessings of prayer into my family's future.

Day 90

Make sure that nobody pays back wrong for wrong, but always strive to do what is good for each other and for everyone else.

1 Thessalonians 5:15 (NIV)

Reflect

When our failings run deep, God's love runs deeper.

Mary C. Neal, M.D.

Act

Close your eyes, breathe deeply, and ask Jesus to reveal His magnificent peace to you.

Pray

Lord, with Your help I will focus on each small step of the climb instead of the mountain that stands before me.

Day 91

Cast all your anxiety on him because he cares for you.

1 Peter 5:7 (NIV)

Reflect

Don't pray when you feel like it. Have an appointment with the Lord and keep it. A man is powerful on his knees.

Corrie ten Boom, writer

Act

Turn to God's Word to live your best life.

Pray

Heavenly Father, use me today to carry Your truth and show Your light.

Day 92

Be on your guard; stand firm in the faith; be courageous; be strong.

1 Corinthians 16:13 (NIV)

Reflect

You are infinitely dear to the Father, unspeakably precious to Him. You are never, not for one second, alone.

Norman F. Dowty, pastor and author

Act

Try something new every day. You never know what you'll end up loving.

Pray

Lord, please give me the courage to take the bold steps required to act.

Day 93

For the LORD is good and his love endures forever; his faithfulness continues through all generations.

Psalm 100:5 (NIV)

Reflect

Happiness isn't something that depends on our surroundings…it's something we make inside ourselves.

Corrie ten Boom, writer

Act

Think of a Jesuslike way to show your love to someone today.

Pray

Dear Lord, help me to remember that the brightness of Your loving presence is always with me.

Day 94

The unfolding of your words gives light; it gives understanding to the simple.

Psalm 119:130 (NIV)

Reflect

I would rather walk with God in the dark than go alone in the light.

Mary Gardiner Brainard, poet

Act

Remember all that Jesus has done for you. Make a time line of the moments that He has come through for you and thank Him for each one.

Pray

Thank You, Lord, for being the light that leads me upward, closer to You.

Day 95

But I trust in you, LORD; I say,
"You are my God."

Psalm 31:14 (NIV)

Reflect

When the world pushes you to your knees,
you're in the perfect position to pray.

Rumi, poet

Act

Don't let your doubts blind you from your goals.

Pray

Nothing is too hard for me, Lord, as long
as it takes me back to You.

Day 96

Give us today our daily bread.

Matthew 6:11 (NIV)

Reflect

Faith is seeing light with your heart when all your eyes see is darkness.

Barbara Johnson, writer

Act

Ask for God's wisdom to guide you right now.

Pray

Heavenly Father, help me to live one day at a time and to trust that You will always provide exactly what I need.

Day 97

For the Spirit God gave us does not make us timid, but gives us power, love and self-discipline.

2 Timothy 1:7 (NIV)

Reflect

Heaven is full of answers to prayer for which no one ever bothered to ask.

Billy Graham

Act

Have great hopes, and dare to go all out for them.

Pray

Lord, I often forget to praise You and thank You for all that You have done for me. Help me to remember to keep my trust in You.

Day 98

David also said to Solomon his son, "Be strong and courageous, and do the work. Do not be afraid or discouraged, for the LORD God, my God, is with you. He will not fail you or forsake you until all the work for the service of the temple of the LORD is finished."

1 Chronicles 28:20 (NIV)

Reflect

Nothing is more important than honesty in prayer. There are no pretensions in prayer, so the best place to begin is wherever you are.

Robert Schuller, pastor, motivational speaker, and author

Act

Rely on your faith during challenging times; be strong and courageous.

Pray

Lord, I pray that I grow closer and closer to You every day.

Day 99

I say to myself, "The Lord is my portion; therefore I will wait for him."

Lamentations 3:24 (NIV)

Reflect

Have courage for the great sorrows of life and patience for the small ones. And when you have finished your daily task, go to sleep in peace. God is awake.

Victor Hugo, writer and politician

Act

Don't focus on your fears or weaknesses. Keep Jesus in mind.

Pray

Father, grant me patience when I stumble and courage to continue on.

Day 100

If your enemy is hungry, feed him; if he is thirsty, give him something to drink. In doing this, you will heap burning coals on his head. Do not be overcome by evil, but overcome evil with good.

Romans 12:20–21 (NIV)

Reflect

I choose love. No occasion justifies hatred; no injustice warrants bitterness, I choose love. Today I will love God and what God loves.

Max Lucado, pastor and author

Act

Today is a gift. Use it to extend your love.

Pray

My Lord, I know that You really do love me. Help me to share my love with others.

Day 101

I will sing of the mercies of the Lord forever; with my mouth will I make known Your faithfulness to all generations.

Psalm 89:1 (NKJV)

Reflect

When you live with hope in your heart, mind, and spirit, you have discovered one of life's most powerful secrets of success.

Norman Vincent Peale, pastor and author

Act

Ask Jesus to shine His light on any area of your life that seems dark and frightening to you.

Pray

Dear God, lead me through today with new insights and new hope.

Day 102

Bearing with one another, and forgiving one another, if anyone has a complaint against another; even as Christ forgave you, so you also must do.

Colossians 3:13 (NIV)

Reflect

Life becomes harder for us when we live for others, but it also becomes richer and happier.

Albert Schweitzer, theologian, philosopher, and physician

Act

Forgive those who have crossed you. Your forgiveness is your most important contribution to the healing of the world.

Pray

Lord, move over my heart and stir up love within it.

Day 103

The minute I said, "I'm slipping, I'm falling," your love, God, took hold and held me fast. When I was upset and beside myself, you calmed me down and cheered me up.

Psalm 94:18–19 (MSG)

Reflect

Something terrible can happen to you, and yet, the day after this something terrible, the sun still rises, and life goes on. And therefore, so must you.

Martin Short, comedian

Act

Instead of taking on a problem by yourself, take a deep breath and remember that God is in control.

Pray

Heavenly Father, please help me truly trust and allow You to guide my life.

Day 104

Light shines on the righteous and joy on the upright in heart.

Psalm 97:11 (NIV)

Reflect

In daily life we must see that it is not happiness that makes us grateful, but gratefulness that makes us happy.

Brother David Steindl-Rast, author, scholar, and Benedictine monk

Act

Offer prayers of gratitude for your blessings.

Pray

Giver of all that is good, how grateful I am for Your abundant kindness.

Day 105

LORD, our Lord, how majestic is your name in all the earth! You have set your glory in the heavens. When I consider your heavens, the work of your fingers, the moon and the stars, which you have set in place, what is mankind that you are mindful of them, human beings that you care for them?

Psalm 8:1, 3–4 (NIV)

Reflect

The miracle of gratitude is that it shifts your perception to such an extent that it changes the world you see.

Robert Holden, psychologist and author

Act

Recognize the infinite possibilities of God's work.

Pray

Dear Lord, when I am focused on my problems and most likely making mountains out of molehills, guide me to go outside, look upward, and have faith in Your omnipotence.

Day 106

In return for my friendship they accuse me, but I am a man of prayer.

Psalm 109:4 (NIV)

Reflect

Prayer—secret, fervent, believing prayer—lies at the root of all personal godliness.

William Carey, missionary

Act

Start a joy journal and log God's goodness daily.

Pray

Lord, thank You for the many ways in which I may lift my heart and spirit through prayer.

Day 107

Blessed are the peacemakers, for they will be called children of God.

Matthew 5:9 (NIV)

Reflect

In a world where you can be anything, be kind.

Seen on a bumper sticker
in Northborough, Massachusetts

Act

Extend a kind hand, a kind word to someone in need.

Pray

Dear Lord, I want to shine Your light. Guide me where I am needed. Give me the grace to be kind and the patience to serve You well.

Day 108

You also must be ready all the time, for the Son of Man will come when least expected.

Luke 12:40 (NLT)

Reflect

Life isn't always about finding yourself.
More often than not, it's about discovering
who God created you to be.

David A. R. White, actor and producer

Act

Consider how different your day would be
if you lived anticipating Christ's return.

Pray

Heavenly Father, help me grow in spirit and
understanding so that I am ready for You.

Day 109

For we believe that Jesus died and rose again, and so we believe that God will bring with Jesus those who have fallen asleep in him.

1 Thessalonians 4:14 (NIV)

Reflect

With the new day comes new strength and new thoughts.

Eleanor Roosevelt

Act

Remember that faith will lead you through unsteady times.

Pray

Lord, peace is knowing that Your comfort is only a prayer away.

Day 110

May the God of hope fill you with all joy and peace as you trust in him, so that you may overflow with hope by the power of the Holy Spirit.

Romans 15:13 (NIV)

Reflect

No matter what has happened to you in the past or what is going on in your life right now, it has no power to keep you from having an amazingly good future if you will walk by faith in God. God loves you! He wants you to live with victory over sin so you can possess His promises for your life today!

Joyce Meyer, author

Act

Focus on your goals and chase away excuses.

Pray

Lord, help me to look to tomorrow with hope.

Day 111

For the Lord your God is the one who goes with you to fight for you against your enemies to give you victory.

Deuteronomy 20:4 (NIV)

Reflect

We can't always withdraw to quiet hillsides to pray, but Christ will meet with us in the quiet places of our hearts.

Sheila Walsh, author

Act

Take comfort knowing God is with you.

Pray

Heavenly Father, help me to hear Your voice deep in my heart, guiding me.

Day 112

I know that you can do all things; no purpose of yours can be thwarted.

Job 42:2 (NIV)

Reflect

Sometimes the Lord rides out the storm with us, and other times He calms the restless sea around us. Most of all, He calms the storm inside us in our deepest inner soul.

Lloyd John Ogilvie, minister

Act

In times of trouble, think of Jesus as your 911.

Pray

Lord, thank You for renewing me and giving me a life that has purpose and meaning.

Day 113

Do nothing out of selfish ambition or vain conceit. Rather, in humility value others above yourselves.

Philippians 2:3 (NIV)

Reflect

Often a healing takes place in ourselves as we pray for the healing of others.

Michael E. DeBakey, surgeon

Act

Guide me, Father, to sow Your seeds in the hearts of others.

Pray

You fill me with concern for others, Lord, and You give me strength to help them.

Day 114

And so we know and rely on the love God has for us. God is love. Whoever lives in love lives in God, and God in them.

1 John 4:16 (NIV)

Reflect

Faith is the root of all blessings. Believe, and you shall be saved.

Jeremy Taylor, author

Act

Ask Jesus for direction as you head into all that awaits you today.

Pray

Oh Lord, teach me to remember You in all things, every day of my life.

Day 115

In your unfailing love you will lead the people you have redeemed. In your strength you will guide them to your holy dwelling.

Exodus 15:13 (NIV)

Reflect

Believe that you can and you're halfway there.

Theodore Roosevelt

Act

Confidently trust God to handle things beyond your efforts.

Pray

Lord, thank You for the mountains, and thank You for walking through the valleys too.

Day 116

Be still before the Lord and wait patiently for him; do not fret when people succeed in their ways, when they carry out their wicked schemes.

Psalm 37:7 (NIV)

Reflect

To pray is to listen, to move through my own chattering to God, to that place where I can be silent and listen to what God may have to say.

Madeleine L'Engle, author

Act

Don't focus on your fears or weaknesses. Keep Jesus in mind.

Pray

Dear God, let me be as quick to forget my troubles as I tend to be at forgetting my blessings. And help me to remember Your goodness always.

Day 117

But as for me, I watch in hope for the Lord, I wait for God my Savior; my God will hear me.

Micah 7:7 (NIV)

Reflect

First thing every morning before you arise, say out loud "I believe" three times.

Norman Vincent Peale, pastor and author

Act

Start another day just right, with a new hope.

Pray

Lord, all things are possible if we believe. Thank You for loving us enough to send what we need.

Day 118

For in this hope we were saved. But hope that is seen is no hope at all. Who hopes for what they already have?

Romans 8:24 (NIV)

Reflect

God never disappoints anyone who places his trust in Him.

Basilea Schlink, religious leader and writer

Act

Do not let fear stop you from reaching your goals.

Pray

Dear Lord, thank You for seasons and restarts and renewed energy. Help me to accomplish something wonderful today.

Day 119

I am the Lord; that is my name!
I will not yield my glory to another
or my praise to idols.

Isaiah 42:8 (NIV)

Reflect

What would our lives look like if we really did live with our life's brevity at the forefront of our mind? Would we pursue the temporary, or would we pursue the eternal?

Julie Manning, author

Act

Surrender your life to God and every experience will grow increasingly more wonderful.

Pray

Dear God, help me to live with a sense of wonder in all of life's experiences.

Day 120

For I am convinced that neither death nor life, neither angels nor demons, neither the present nor the future, nor any powers, neither height nor depth, nor anything else in all creation, will be able to separate us from the love of God that is in Christ Jesus our Lord.

Romans 8:38–39 (NIV)

Reflect

There is no one who is insignificant in the purpose of God.

Alistair Begg, pastor

Act

Lead me today, Lord, so that I follow Your will.

Pray

Father, let me seek You as eagerly as I seek those here on earth who love me.

Day 121

For the eyes of the LORD are on the righteous and his ears are attentive to their prayer, but the face of the LORD is against those who do evil.

1 Peter 3:12 (NIV)

Reflect

There is always the danger that we may just do the work for the sake of the work. This is where the respect and the love and the devotion come in—that we do it to God, to Christ, and that's why we try to do it as beautifully as possible.

Mother Teresa

Act

Place your hope and purpose completely in God's hands.

Pray

Lord, remove my fear and help me to trust in You and take You at Your word.

Day 122

And let us run with perseverance the race marked out for us, fixing our eyes on Jesus, the pioneer and perfecter of faith. For the joy set before him he endured the cross, scorning its shame, and sat down at the right hand of the throne of God.

Hebrews 12:1–2 (NIV)

Reflect

When you cannot stand, He will bear you in His arms.

Saint Francis de Sales

Act

Cultivate your relationship with Christ.

Pray

Help me to trust You in all things, Lord, and to leave the results to You.

Day 123

Be strong and courageous. Do not be afraid or terrified because of them, for the Lord your God goes with you; he will never leave you nor forsake you.

Deuteronomy 31:6 (NIV)

Reflect

Go where your best prayers take you.

Frederick Buechner, writer

Act

Remember that remarkable achievements begin as thoughts.

Pray

My heavenly Father, from whom I have received every good and perfect gift, thank You.

Day 124

And the seed that fell on good soil represents those who hear and accept God's word and produce a harvest of thirty, sixty, or even a hundred times as much as had been planted!

Mark 4:20 (NLT)

Reflect

Disappointments are just God's way of saying, "I've got something better." So be patient, have faith, and live your life.

Anonymous

Act

Write down five blessings or answers to prayer that Jesus has bestowed upon you this week.

Pray

Father, help me to remember Your goodness and grace every day.

Day 125

But blessed are your eyes because they see, and your ears because they hear.

Matthew 13:16 (NIV)

Reflect

Do not turn me into restless waters if you cannot promise to be my stream.

Sanober Khan, poet and writer

Act

Lean on the One who cares.

Pray

Dear Savior, though words alone can never do justice to the grace You have shown me, I want to say thank You for Your great salvation and love.

Day 126

Yet to all who did receive him, to those who believed in his name, he gave the right to become children of God.

John 1:12 (NIV)

Reflect

Prayer is the pulse of life.

Andrew Murray, writer and pastor

Act

Take stock of your life. Take time to thank Jesus for giving you everything that you need.

Pray

Lord, thank You for being the ultimate provider.

Day 127

Whoever is kind to the poor lends to the LORD, and he will reward them for what they have done.

Proverbs 19:17 (NIV)

Reflect

Sometimes God redeems your story by surrounding you with people who need to hear your past so it doesn't become their future.

Jon Acuff, author

Act

Reach out and help someone by sharing your love and time.

Pray

Father, may my gifts to others reflect Your timeless love.

Day 128

If you falter in a time of trouble, how small is your strength!

Proverbs 24:10 (NIV)

Reflect

The opposite of joy is not sorrow. It is unbelief.

Leslie Weatherhead, theologian

Act

Relax and accept God's grace in times of stress.

Pray

Father, thank You for the opportunities of renewal You grant me each and every day.

Day 129

"I tell you the truth," Jesus said, "this poor widow has given more than all the rest of them."

Luke 21:3 (NLT)

Reflect

Gentleness, self-sacrifice, and generosity are the exclusive possession of no one race or religion.

Mahatma Gandhi

Act

Ask Jesus to show you new ways to find joy in serving.

Pray

Lord, thank You for the gift-givers who have enriched my life. May I in turn bless others.

Day 130

I love those who love me, and those who seek me find me.

Proverbs 8:17 (NIV)

Reflect

Prayer enlarges the heart until it is capable of containing God's gift of Himself.

Mother Teresa

Act

Be an instrument of God's love in this world.

Pray

Lord, in all the times and places of my life, Your love never leaves me.

Day 131

Because you know that the testing of your faith produces perseverance.

James 1:3 (NIV)

Reflect

I can safely say, on the authority of all that is revealed in the Word of God, that any man or woman on this earth who is bored and turned off by worship is not ready for heaven.

A. W. Tozer, pastor and author

Act

Diminish doubt and increase your faith.

Pray

Fill me with trust, O Holy Spirit,
and increase my faith.

Day 132

Whoever dwells in the shelter of the Most High will rest in the shadow of the Almighty.

Psalm 91:1 (NIV)

Reflect

God does not give us everything we want, but He does fulfill His promises, leading us along the best and straightest paths to Himself.

Dietrich Bonhoeffer

Act

Know that though you may have difficulties, you will be able to handle all of them, for God will give His angels charge over you.

Pray

Heavenly Father, I will write this psalm on my heart so that no matter how hard my life may be, I will always be on top of things.

Day 133

Those who sacrifice thank offerings honor me, and to the blameless I will show my salvation.

Psalm 50:23 (NIV)

Reflect

Look for yourself, and you will find in the long run only hatred, loneliness, despair, rage, ruin, and decay. But look for Christ, and you will find Him, and with Him everything else thrown in.

C. S. Lewis, theologian and writer

Act

Give away a treasured belonging as an act of worship to Jesus.

Pray

Heavenly Father, guide my words and actions by Your pure love.

Day 134

I am with you and will watch over you wherever you go, and I will bring you back to this land. I will not leave you until I have done what I have promised you.

Genesis 28:15 (NIV)

Reflect

Say you are well, or all is well with you, and God shall hear your words and make them true.

Ella Wheeler Wilcox, author

Act

Create positive messages that will forever resonate your beauty.

Pray

Lord, help me to see the blessings that might come from my difficulties.

Day 135

Greater love has no one than this: to lay down one's life for one's friends.

John 15:13 (NIV)

Reflect

Courage is contagious. When a brave man takes a stand, the spines of others are often stiffened.

Billy Graham

Act

Remember all those who bravely gave their lives for their country.

Pray

Dear Lord, thank You for the dedicated men and women who serve in our armed forces. We pause in remembrance of those who have gone before them, often serving in harm's way to protect the liberties we enjoy today.

Day 136

When he brings out his own sheep, he goes before them; and the sheep follow him, for they know his voice.

John 10:4 (NKJV)

Reflect

Never doubt in the darkness what God has given us in the light.

Francine Rivers, author

Act

Surrender to the moment and recognize every challenge is an opportunity for personal growth.

Pray

Keep me close to You, Lord. Replace my sorrow with the warmth of Your comfort.

Day 137

In all this you greatly rejoice, though now for a little while you may have had to suffer grief in all kinds of trials.

1 Peter 1:6 (NIV)

Reflect

The highest form of thinking is prayer.

Norman Vincent Peale, pastor and author

Act

Open your heart and invite Jesus in.

Pray

Thank You, Jesus, for the precious moments when You bless my worship with Your Holy Spirit.

Day 138

I always thank my God as I remember you in my prayers.

Philemon 1:4 (NIV)

Reflect

We never test the resources of God until we attempt the impossible.

F. B. Meyer, pastor

Act

Ask God to strengthen you by the power of His might.

Pray

Thank You, Lord, for the unexpected good things that happen to us.

Day 139

Seek the Lord while He may be found,
call upon Him while He is near.

Isaiah 55:6 (NKJV)

Reflect

God takes life's pieces and gives us
unbroken peace.

W. D. Gough, poet

Act

Share a hope-building story with someone today.

Pray

Heavenly Father, thank You for walking with us
through all of life's difficult circumstances. Help us
remember to share with others what You have done.

Day 140

I thank my God every time I remember you. In all my prayers for all of you, I always pray with joy.

Philippians 1:3–4 (NIV)

Reflect

We walk without fear, full of hope and courage and strength to do His will, waiting for the endless good which He is always giving as fast as He can get us able to take it in.

George MacDonald, minister, author, and poet

Act

Recognize that your faith will lead you to great things.

Pray

Dear Lord, thank You for giving me the strength to withstand difficulties.

Day 141

"For I know the plans I have for you," declares the Lord, "plans to prosper you and not to harm you, plans to give you hope and a future."

Jeremiah 29:11 (NIV)

Reflect

Each of us, made in His image and likeness, is yet another promise He has made to the universe that He will continue to love it and care for it.

Brennan Manning, priest and author

Act

Stand outside this evening. Look at the stars. Know that you are special and loved by the One who created them.

Pray

God, help me to recognize Your influence in my life.

Day 142

As iron sharpens iron, so a person sharpens his friend.

Proverbs 27:17 (NET)

Reflect

I cannot even imagine where I would be today were it not for that handful of friends who have given me a heart full of joy. Let's face it, friends make life a lot more fun.

Charles R. Swindoll, pastor and author

Act

Write an encouraging note to a friend, thanking them for their gift of friendship.

Pray

Thank You, Lord, for moving me out of my comfort zone and planting precious friends along the way.

Day 143

Whatever you do, work at it with all your heart, as working for the LORD, not for human masters.

Colossians 3:23 (NIV)

Reflect

Every day we live is a priceless gift of God, loaded with possibilities to learn something new, to gain fresh insights.

Dale Evans Rogers, singer

Act

Encourage me, God, to see the value in what I have.

Pray

Dear God, lead me through today with new insights and new hope.

Day 144

Rather, as servants of God we commend ourselves in every way: in great endurance; in troubles, hardships and distresses.

2 Corinthians 6:4 (NIV)

Reflect

He who has God and everything has no more than he who has God alone.

C. S. Lewis, theologian and writer

Act

Build your life on the foundation of faith.

Pray

Thank You, Lord, that You know our needs and are always ready to meet them.

Day 145

Let us come before him with thanksgiving and extol him with music and song.

Psalm 95:2 (NIV)

Reflect

All the world is an utterance of the Almighty.
Its countless beauties, its exquisite adaptations,
all speak to you of Him.

Phillips Brooks, clergyman and author

Act

Open your heart to the beauty that surrounds you.

Pray

Dear Lord, please help me to see the
beauty of every day.

Day 146

**Search me, God, and know my heart;
test me and know my anxious thoughts.
See if there is any offensive way in me,
and lead me in the way everlasting.**

Psalm 139:23–24 (NIV)

Reflect

Faith is a living, daring confidence in God's grace, so sure and certain that a man could stake his life on it a thousand times.

Martin Luther, priest

Act

When life feels desperate, look for signs of Jesus's grace.

Pray

Lord, help me understand the eternal truth that You are with us at every turn.

Day 147

I keep my eyes always on the Lord. With him at my right hand, I will not be shaken.

Psalm 16:8 (NIV)

Reflect

God's mercies are new every morning.
Receive them.

Max Lucado, pastor and author

Act

Take comfort knowing God is with you.

Pray

Dear Lord, remind me to rest in Your presence and in the knowledge that You are working everything out according to Your plan.

Day 148

If you declare with your mouth, "Jesus is LORD," and believe in your heart that God raised him from the dead, you will be saved.

Romans 10:9 (NIV)

Reflect

Every morning I spend fifteen minutes filling my mind full of God; and so there's no room left for worry thoughts.

Howard Chandler Christy, artist

Act

Remember your faith is the best answer to anxiety.

Pray

Lord, when I am full of fear and worry help me to take my eyes off of myself and to focus on You.

Day 149

Every good and perfect gift is from above, coming down from the Father of the heavenly lights, who does not change like shifting shadows.

James 1:17 (NIV)

Reflect

Trust in the Redeemer's strength...exercise what faith you have, and by and by He shall rise upon you with healing beneath His wings. Go from faith to faith and you shall receive blessing upon blessing.

Charles H. Spurgeon, preacher

Act

Think of your day as a channel for God's blessings.

Pray

Thank You, Lord, for Your many blessings, but especially for the love that makes all of us one family in You.

Day 150

Be reconciled with Him, and be at peace; thereby good will come to you.

Job 22:21 (NASB)

Reflect

I expect the best and with God's help will attain the best.

Norman Vincent Peale, pastor and author

Act

Agree to open your life to His touch, and you will receive His power and abundance.

Pray

Heavenly Father, I am amazed at the marvelous things You can do when I yield myself to You.

Day 151

**Holy, holy, holy is the LORD of hosts;
the whole earth is full of His glory!"**

Isaiah 6:3 (NKJV)

Reflect

In God's wisdom, He frequently chooses to meet our needs by showing His love toward us through the hands and hearts of others.

Jack Hayford, minister and author

Act

Today, let go of judgment and reach out to others in need. Offer them prayer.

Pray

God, guide me to see the people in my life just as You created them.

Day 152

**The LORD make His face shine upon you,
and be gracious to you.**

Numbers 6:5 (NKJV)

Reflect

Look deep within yourself and recognize
what brings life and grace into your heart....
You are loved by God.

Christopher de Vinck, author

Act

Relax and accept God's grace in times of stress.

Pray

Dear Lord, I am grateful for the love
You have given me.

Day 153

I pray that out of his glorious riches he may strengthen you with power through his Spirit in your inner being, so that Christ may dwell in your hearts through faith.

Ephesians 3:16–17 (NIV)

Reflect

I can see, and that is why I can be happy, in what you call the dark, but which to me is golden. I can see a God-made world, not a manmade world.

Helen Keller

Act

When your phone or other device pings you today, pause long enough to check your connection with the messages Jesus is sending.

Pray

Lord, make my heart a dwelling place where You truly feel at home.

Day 154

Now this is the confidence that we have in Him, that if we ask anything according to His will, He hears us.

1 John 5:14 (NKJV)

Reflect

You can see God from anywhere if your mind is set to love and obey Him.

A. W. Tozer, pastor and author

Act

Turn to God and draw upon His incomparable wisdom.

Pray

Heavenly Father, keep my spirit open today to the power of Your guidance and strength.

Day 155

I will refresh the weary and satisfy the faint.

Jeremiah 31:25 (NIV)

Reflect

If the Lord be with us, we have no cause to fear. His eye is upon us, His arm over us, His ear open to our prayer.

Andrew Murray, writer and pastor

Act

Open your front door and ask God to come in. Thank Him for being with you in everything you do.

Pray

Lord, You know my fears. Please give me the courage to do what I fear I can't.

Day 156

And we know that in all things God works for the good of those who love him, who have been called according to his purpose.

Romans 8:28 (NIV)

Reflect

I do not want to foresee the future. I am concerned with taking care of the present. God has given me no control over the moment following.

Mahatma Gandhi

Act

Dear Lord, guide me toward Your plan.
Help me to take the first step.

Pray

Lord, help me to find the place where
You can use me best.

Day 157

This is love: not that we loved God, but that he loved us and sent his Son as an atoning sacrifice for our sins.

1 John 4:10 (NIV)

Reflect

Spread love everywhere you go. Let no one ever come to you without leaving happier.

Mother Teresa

Act

Love yourself first and everything else will fall into line.

Pray

Dear God, help me to see glimpses of Your love throughout my day and to smile and thank You.

Day 158

He said to them, "Follow me, ad I will make you fishers of men." Immediately they left their nets and followed him.

Matthew 4:19–20 (ESV)

Reflect

Miracles are of all sizes. And if you start believing in little miracles, you can work up to the bigger ones.

Norman Vincent Peale, pastor and author

Act

Ask Jesus to lead you, then watch for the ways He guides your path.

Pray

Dear Lord, help us hunger for Your wisdom, Your guidance, and Your joy.

Day 159

I press on toward the goal to win the prize for which God has called me heavenward in Christ Jesus.

Philippians 3:14 (NIV)

Reflect

Your potential is the sum of all the possibilities God has for your life.

Charles Stanley, pastor

Act

Realize that in order to discover your true potential, you must help others discover theirs.

Pray

Heavenly Father, keep my spirit open today to the power of Your guidance and strength.

Day 160

Whether you turn to the right or to the left, your ears will hear a voice behind you saying, "This is the way; walk in it."

Isaiah 30:1 (NIV)

Reflect

Pursue some path, however narrow and crooked, in which you can walk with love and reverence.

Henry David Thoreau, poet and philosopher

Act

Ask Jesus to direct any decision you need to make today.

Pray

Lord, help me to see the imprint of Your hand on my life and to order my steps according to Your plan.

Day 161

Above all else, guard your heart, for everything you do flows from it.

Proverbs 4:23 (NIV)

Reflect

Trials...may come in abundance. But they cannot penetrate into the sanctuary of the soul when it is settled in God, and we may dwell in perfect peace.

Hannah Whitall Smith, author

Act

What is holding you captive? Your job? Financial worries? A past sin? Know that there is freedom in Jesus.

Pray

Assure us, Lord, in darkest distress that trials don't mean You love us less.

Day 162

And the God of all grace, who called you to his eternal glory in Christ, after you have suffered a little while, will himself restore you and make you strong, firm and steadfast.

1 Peter 5:10 (NIV)

Reflect

Kites rise highest against the wind—not with it.

Winston Churchill

Act

Take comfort knowing God is with you.

Pray

Father, even in difficult times, remind us to trust in You and cling to Your Word for encouragement.

Day 163

Congenial conversation—what a pleasure! The right word at the right time—beautiful!

Proverbs 15:23 (MSG)

Reflect

We're prone to want God to change our circumstances, but He wants to change our character. We think that peace comes from the outside in, but it comes from the inside out.

Warren W. Wiersbe, clergyman and writer

Act

Lord, direct me toward peace.

Pray

Lord of all times and circumstances, thank You for life lessons from the past.

Day 164

The light shines in the darkness, and the darkness has not overcome it.

John 1:5 (NIV)

Reflect

There is nothing anybody else can do that can stop God from using us. We can turn everything into a testimony.

Corrie ten Boom, writer

Act

Use the difficulties in your life to increase your ability to love.

Pray

Oh, Father, help me remember that I can't go anywhere without You.

Day 165

May he endure as long as the sun, as long as the moon, through all generations.

Psalm 72:5 (NIV)

Reflect

Have patience. There is no time that is not God's time.

Criswell Freeman, psychologist and author

Act

Offer prayers of gratitude for your blessings.

Pray

Teach me to be thankful at all times, Lord.

Day 166

My intercessor is my friend as my eyes pour out tears to God; on behalf of a man he pleads with God as one pleads for a friend.

Job 16:20–21 (NIV)

Reflect

Be with someone who brings out the best in you, not the stress in you.

Anonymous

Act

Grasp every opportunity to offer encouragement to others.

Pray

Mistakes are never the end of the line with You, God. Thank You for Your forgiveness, the ultimate eraser.

Day 167

I know that there is nothing better for people than to be happy and to do good while they live. That each of them may eat and drink, and find satisfaction in all their toil—this is the gift of God.

Ecclesiastes 3:12–13 (NIV)

Reflect

A man who is intimate with God will never be intimidated by men.

Leonard Ravenhill, author

Act

Strengthen your friendship with Jesus by sharing your heart's desires with Him today.

Pray

Lord, thank You for the grace that strengthens me for tasks large and small.

Day 168

You will keep in perfect peace those whose minds are steadfast, because they trust in you.

Isaiah 26:3 (NIV)

Reflect

Prayer is not asking for what you think you want, but asking to be changed in ways you can't imagine.

Kathleen Norris, poet

Act

Always look to your heart for the true answer.

Pray

Lord, You are the answer to all of my questions.

Day 169

Do not swerve to the right or to the left; turn your foot away from evil.

Proverbs 4:27 (ESV)

Reflect

The fact that I can plant a seed and it becomes a flower, share a bit of knowledge and it becomes another's, smile at someone and receive a smile in return, are to me continual spiritual exercises.

Leo Buscaglia, author and motivational speaker

Act

Ask Jesus to keep you on the good road.

Pray

Lord, help me eject from my heart the things that harm me and separate me from You.

Day 170

Come to me, all you who are weary and burdened, and I will give you rest.

Matthew 11:28 (NIV)

Reflect

Never be in a hurry; do everything quietly and in a calm spirit. Do not lose your inner peace for anything whatsoever, even if your whole world seems upset.

Saint Francis de Sales

Act

Give thought and thanks for the light of day and the comfort of night.

Pray

God, calm my fears and give me peace.

Day 171

Being confident of this, that he who began a good work in you will carry it on to completion until the day of Christ Jesus.

Philippians 1:6 (NIV)

Reflect

Trust is the glue of life. It's the most essential ingredient in effective communication. It's the foundational principle that holds all relationships.

Stephen Covey, educator and author

Act

Today listen to that quiet voice, and hear the simple words Jesus speaks: Trust Me.

Pray

Lord, thank You for knowing my heart's deepest needs and desires even better than I do. Today let me put all my hope in You and wait patiently for Your answers.

Day 172

So do not be afraid of them, for there is nothing concealed that will not be disclosed, or hidden that will not be made known.

Matthew 10:26 (NIV)

Reflect

Greatness is not measured by what a man or woman accomplishes, but by the opposition he or she has overcome to reach his goals.

Dorothy Height,
civil rights and women's rights activist

Act

View your problems with a spiritual perspective.

Pray

Thank You, Lord, for the tremendous difference You make in our lives.

Day 173

Jesus looked at them and said, "With man this is impossible, but not with God; all things are possible with God."

Mark 10:27 (NIV)

Reflect

Start by doing what's necessary; then do what's possible; and suddenly you are doing the impossible.

Saint Francis of Assisi

Act

Imagine the impossible.

Pray

Lord, keep me true to the beauty with which You created me.

Day 174

Peace I leave with you; my peace I give you. I do not give to you as the world gives. Do not let your hearts be troubled and do not be afraid.

John 14:27 (NIV)

Reflect

Sometimes the Lord rides out the storm with us and other times He calms the restless sea around us. Most of all, He calms the storm inside us in our deepest inner soul.

Lloyd John Ogilvie, minister

Act

When fear comes, counter it with an affirmation of faith.

Pray

My Lord God, I have no idea where I am going. I do not see the road ahead of me. Help me remember that You will lead me by the right road, though I may know nothing about it.

Day 175

The Spirit gives life; the flesh counts for nothing. The words I have spoken to you—they are full of the Spirit and life.

John 6:63 (NIV)

Reflect

Time is too slow for those who wait, too swift for those who fear, too long for those who grieve, too short for those who rejoice, but for those who love, time is eternity.

Henry Van Dyke, author, educator, and clergyman

Act

Commit to work toward the goal of relishing the simple things.

Pray

Lord, open my eyes to the love around me, and help me see how much You love me through others.

Day 176

I saw a light from heaven, brighter than the sun, blazing around me and my companions.

Acts 26:13 (NIV)

Reflect

One's life has value so long as one attributes value to the life of others, by means of love, friendship, indignation, and compassion.

Simone de Beauvoir, philosopher and writer

Act

Ask Jesus to put a person on your heart who needs His love, then pray for that person throughout the day.

Pray

Lord, light up the world so I can see others through Your eyes.

Day 177

Again, truly I tell you that if two of you on earth agree about anything they ask for, it will be done for them by my Father in heaven.

Matthew 18:19 (NIV)

Reflect

Make no mistake about it, responsibilities toward other human beings are the greatest blessings God can send us.

Dorothy Dix, journalist

Act

Cherish your purpose in life.

Pray

Lord, keep me alert for opportunities to ease another's suffering.

Day 178

But Jesus, knowing their thoughts, said, "Why do you think evil in your hearts?"

Matthew 9:4 (NKJV)

Reflect

Life is not easy for any of us. But what of that? We must have perseverance and above all confidence in ourselves. We must believe that we are gifted for something and that this thing must be attained.

Marie Curie, physicist

Act

Tell Jesus about a tough issue you're facing, then listen for His still small voice.

Pray

Jesus, help me be still and listen when You talk to me.

Day 179

Do not forget to entertain strangers, for by so doing some have unwittingly entertained angels.

Hebrews 13:2 (NKJV)

Reflect

If you begin to live life looking for the God that is all around you, every moment becomes a prayer.

Frank Bianco, seminarian and journalist

Act

Find a way to be a loving presence and reflect the peace of Christ today.

Pray

Lord, let me always remember that Your Word teaches me to welcome strangers.

Day 180

Above all else, guard your heart, for everything you do flows from it.

Proverbs 4:23 (NIV)

Reflect

You can't have a better tomorrow if you're thinking about yesterday.

Charles Kettering, inventor

Act

Waste no tears over yesterday's grief.

Pray

Dear Lord, You are my foundation, yesterday, today, and forever.

Day 181

Can you discover the depths of God? Can you discover the limits of the Almighty?

Job 11:7 (NASB)

Reflect

Life itself is the most wonderful fairy tale.

Hans Christian Andersen, author

Act

Take a walk and notice life growing from a plant. Thank Jesus for producing new blossoms in your life.

Pray

Lord, thank You for the majesty, mystery, and grace of life and a beating heart.

Day 182

I sought the Lord, and he answered me; he delivered me from all my fears.

Psalm 34:4 (NIV)

Reflect

God will meet you where you are in order to take you where He wants you to go.

Tony Evans, pastor and author

Act

Ask Jesus to do something so big that when it happens, you'll know it came from Him.

Pray

Oh, Lord, teach me to remember You in all things, every day of my life.

Day 183

And when you stand praying, if you hold anything against anyone, forgive them, so that your Father in heaven may forgive you your sins.

Mark 11:25 (NIV)

Reflect

Not only do we not know God except through Jesus Christ; we do not even know ourselves except through Jesus Christ.

Blaise Pascal, mathematician, inventor, and philosopher

Act

Allow yourself to be loved and to love all who you meet.

Pray

Lord, Your unending forgiveness is balm to my soul. Thank You for transforming my life.

Day 184

For where your treasure is, there your heart will be also.

Matthew 6:21 (ESV)

Reflect

Saying thank you is more than good manners. It is good spirituality.

William Painter, inventor

Act

Share your care and appreciation for a beloved friend by sending a thank-you note and expressing your gratitude.

Pray

Lord, thank You for the many ways in which I may lift my heart and spirit through prayer.

Day 185

For the Father loves the Son and shows him all that he himself is doing. And greater works than these will he show him, so that you may marvel.

John 5:20 (ESV)

Reflect

I don't think that we're meant to understand it all the time. I think that sometimes we just have to have faith.

Nicholas Sparks, author

Act

Surrender your life to God and every experience will grow increasingly more wonderful.

Pray

Lord, thank You for my body in all its amazing and miraculous workings.

Day 186

Usually no one will hurt you for wanting to do good. But even if they should, you are to be envied, for God will reward you for it.

1 Peter 3:13–14 (TLB)

Reflect

We may ignore, but we can nowhere evade the presence of God. The world is crowded with Him. He walks everywhere incognito.

C. S. Lewis, theologian and writer

Act

Ask Jesus to show you how to use your creativity to bless your family, church, or community.

Pray

Father, may my prayers for others be as constant and natural as breathing.

Day 187

Timely advice is as lovely as gold apples in a silver basket.

Proverbs 25:11 (TLB)

Reflect

Every happening, great and small, is a parable whereby God speaks to us, and the art of life is to get the message.

Malcolm Muggeridge, journalist

Act

Put your problems in God's hands.

Pray

Lord, help us to trust You as we walk through our lives.

Day 188

This is the message we have heard from him and declare to you: God is light; in him there is no darkness at all.

1 John 1:5 (NIV)

Reflect

I would rather walk with God in the dark than go alone in the light.

Mary Gardiner Brainard, author and poet

Act

Fill your mind with Christ.

Pray

Lord, thank You for reminding me that when circumstances don't go my way, You could be leading me Your way.

Day 189

Take my yoke upon you and learn from me, for I am gentle and humble in heart, and you will find rest for your souls.

Matthew 11:29 (NIV)

Reflect

No pillow so soft as God's promise.

Author Unknown

Act

Turn to Jesus in your thoughts. He will give you rest.

Pray

Father, restore my soul through deep and abiding rest.

Day 190

He is your praise. He is your God, who has done for you these great and terrifying things that your eyes have seen.

Deuteronomy 10:21 (ESV)

Reflect

I believe in Christianity as I believe that the sun has risen: not only because I see it, but because by it I see everything else.

C. S. Lewis, theologian and writer

Act

Build your life on the foundation of faith.

Pray

Today God, let me shine for You.

Day 191

But seek first his kingdom and his righteousness, and all these things will be given to you as well.

Matthew 6:33 (NIV)

Reflect

Frequently remind yourself that God is with you, that He will never fail you, that you can count upon Him. Say these words, God is with me, helping me.

Norman Vincent Peale, pastor and author

Act

Expect great things to happen.

Pray

Lord, thank You for the grace that strengthens me for tasks large and small.

Day 192

Some trust in chariots and some in horses, but we trust in the name of the LORD our God.

Psalm 20:7 (NIV)

Reflect

Never be afraid to trust an unknown future to a known God.

Corrie ten Boom, writer

Act

Rejoice, for the future is full of promise.

Pray

Father, I hold tight to Your truth and trust You to work in my life.

Day 193

Many are the woes of the wicked, but the Lord's unfailing love surrounds the one who trusts in him.

Psalm 32:10 (NIV)

Reflect

Faith is about doing. You are how you act, not just how you believe.

Mitch Albom, author

Act

Take time to regularly connect with God throughout your day.

Pray

Lord, help me be an example to those around me today, one worth emulating.

Day 194

**Look to the LORD and his strength;
seek his face always.**

1 Chronicles 16:11 (NIV)

Reflect

Faith is for that which lies on the other side of reason. Faith is what makes life bearable, with all its tragedies and ambiguities and sudden, startling joys.

Madeleine L'Engle, author

Act

Learn the great art of doing the best you can, with what you have, where you are.

Pray

Open my eyes, Father, to Your world filled with surprises.

Day 195

Jesus said to him, "If you believe, all things are possible to him who believes."

Mark 9:23 (NKJV)

Reflect

Go where your best prayers take you.

Frederick Buechner, writer

Act

Think prosperity, abundance, and the best of everything. God wants to give to you, His child, every good thing.

Pray

Dear God, help me to recognize Your answers to my prayers.

Day 196

We desire that each one of you show the same diligence to the full assurance of hope until the end, that you do not become sluggish, but imitate those who through faith and patience inherit the promises.

Hebrews 6:11–12 (NKJV)

Reflect

God and Nature first made us what we are, and then out of our own created genius we make ourselves what we want to be. Follow always that great law. Let the sky and God be our limit and Eternity our measurement.

Marcus Garvey, activist and publisher

Act

Ask Jesus to give you clear commands to follow Him.

Pray

Father, even when my legs grow weary, help me to remember to run to You.

Day 197

My dear brothers and sisters, take note of this: Everyone should be quick to listen, slow to speak and slow to become angry.

James 1:19 (NIV)

Reflect

I believe that appreciation is a holy thing, that when we look for what's best in the person we happen to be with at the moment, we're doing what God does; so in appreciating our neighbor, we're participating in something truly sacred.

Mister Rogers

Act

Offer prayers of gratitude for your blessings.

Pray

Thank You, my Lord, for this wonderful life and the wisdom to appreciate it.

Day 198

No temptation has overtaken you except what is common to mankind. And God is faithful; he will not let you be tempted beyond what you can bear. But when you are tempted, he will also provide a way out so that you can endure it.

1 Corinthians 10:13 (NIV)

Reflect

Remember who you are. Don't compromise for anyone, for any reason. You are a child of the Almighty God. Live that truth.

Lysa Terkeurst, author

Act

Work with faithfulness and a grateful heart.

Pray

Heavenly Father, help me release feelings and thoughts that are holding me back from becoming all I am meant to be.

Day 199

When they were discouraged, I smiled and that encouraged them and lightened their spirits.

Job 29:24 (TLB)

Reflect

From quiet homes and first beginning, out to the undiscovered ends, there's nothing worth the wear of winning, but laughter and the love of friends.

Hilaire Belloc, writer and historian

Act

Listen to a Christian comedian online.

Pray

Thank You, Father, for the gift of laughter that heals hearts and heads alike.

Day 200

When you ask, you do not receive, because you ask with wrong motives, that you may spend what you get on your pleasures.

James 4:3 (NIV)

Reflect

If you know that God loves you, you should never question a directive from Him.

Henry Blackaby, pastor and author

Act

As you pray imagine you are talking into a powerful cell phone, built into your head, that can reach heaven on a moment's notice.

Pray

Father, thank You for the gifts You've placed in my heart to give. May they be a blessing to this world and a testament of Your love.

Day 201

Therefore do not worry about tomorrow, for tomorrow will worry about itself. Each day has enough trouble of its own.

Matthew 6:34 (NIV)

Reflect

Stand up to your obstacles and do something about them. You will find that they haven't half the strength you think they have.

Norman Vincent Peale, pastor and author

Act

When fear comes, counter it with an affirmation of faith.

Pray

Vanquish our doubts, Lord, and fill our hearts with faith and trust in You.

Day 202

Give, and it will be given to you. A good measure, pressed down, shaken together and running over, will be poured into your lap. For with the measure you use, it will be measured to you.

Luke 6:38 (NIV)

Reflect

God allows us to experience the low points of life in order to teach us lessons that we could learn in no other way.

C. S. Lewis, theologian and writer

Act

Visualize the protection of being in God's care.

Pray

Heavenly Father, I can endure any situation because I know You are working on my behalf. I'm safe in Your hands.

Day 203

I will hear what God the LORD will speak, for He will speak peace to His people and to His saints; but let them not turn back to folly.

Psalm 85:8 (NKJV)

Reflect

Every moment you get is a gift. Spend it on things that matter. Don't spend it by dwelling on unhappy things.

Celestine Chua, life coach and blogger

Act

Keep alert for any unexpected path Jesus wants you to follow. Someone may be expecting you.

Pray

Lord, in all the times and places of my life, Your love never leaves me.

Day 204

He will be eating curds and honey when he knows enough to reject the wrong and choose the right.

Isaiah 7:15 (NIV)

Reflect

I believe God embedded the miraculous in the ordinary, and it is our task to discover it and celebrate it.

Kent Nerburn, author

Act

When you are full of fear, confused, out of control, filled with doubt, or so busy you can barely see straight, know He is there to guide you.

Pray

Help me to trust You in all things, Lord, and to leave the results to You.

Day 205

For who is God besides the Lord? And who is the Rock except our God?

Psalm 18:31 (NIV)

Reflect

Do kindly things for people, for nothing can so completely erase gloom and create new vigor as the practice of caring and good will.

Norman Vincent Peale, pastor and author

Act

Fill your heart with strength and love for each other.

Pray

Dear Lord, help me to remain watchful and ready to serve others in Your name.

Day 206

Fixing our eyes on Jesus, the pioneer and perfecter of faith. For the joy set before him he endured the cross, scorning its shame, and sat down at the right hand of the throne of God.

Hebrews 12:2 (NIV)

Reflect

Faith is belief in what you cannot see or prove or touch. Faith is walking face-first and full-speed into the dark.

Elizabeth Gilbert, author

Act

Contemplate new ways to extend your voice and bring beauty to the world.

Pray

Lord, help me to be a faithful steward of all the life that surrounds me.

Day 207

You came near when I called you, and you said, "Do not fear."

Lamentations 3:57 (NIV)

Reflect

Every morning I spend fifteen minutes filling my mind full of God, and so there's no room left for worry thoughts.

Howard Chandler Christy, artist

Act

Remember your faith is the best answer to anxiety.

Pray

Lord, when I am full of fear and worry help me to take my eyes off of myself and to focus on You.

Day 208

As the body without the spirit is dead, so faith without deeds is dead.

James 2:26 (NIV)

Reflect

Keep some room in your heart for the unimaginable.

Mary Oliver, poet

Act

Today consider the spiritual gifts God gave you—the unique and precious talents that you bring to the world. Be a light to those around you and bring glory to God.

Pray

Thank You, Lord, that You know our needs and are always ready to meet them.

Day 209

A generous person will prosper; whoever refreshes others will be refreshed.

Proverbs 11:25 (NIV)

Reflect

I used to ask God to help me. Then I asked if I might help Him. I ended up by asking God to do His work through me.

Hudson Taylor, Christian missionary

Act

Be the subtle voice that helps another in need.

Pray

Dear Lord, help me to remember that the brightness of Your loving presence is always with me.

Day 210

But the fruit of the Spirit is love, joy, peace, forbearance, kindness, goodness, faithfulness, gentleness and self-control. Against such things there is no law.

Galatians 5:22–23 (NIV)

Reflect

The most important thing in life is to learn how to give out love, and to let it come in.

Mitch Albom, author

Act

Love one another as He loves us.

Pray

You fill me with concern for others, Lord, and You give me strength to help them.

Day 211

Then Jesus told his disciples a parable to show them that they should always pray and not give up.

Luke 18:1 (NIV)

Reflect

Faith is the most powerful of all forces operating in humanity and when you have it in depth nothing can get you down.

Norman Vincent Peale, pastor and author

Act

Remember that faith will lead you through unsteady times.

Pray

Lord, peace is knowing that Your comfort is only a prayer away.

Day 212

Your love, Lord, reaches to the heavens, your faithfulness to the skies.

Psalm 36:5 (NIV)

Reflect

We must accept finite disappointment, but never lose infinite hope.

Martin Luther King, Jr.

Act

Hold onto God's promises—they will protect you from fear and lead you to joy.

Pray

Dear Lord, help me to begin today with hope, to feel Your love and know I am never alone.

Day 213

In the same way, the Spirit helps us in our weakness. We do not know what we ought to pray for, but the Spirit himself intercedes for us through wordless groans.

Romans 8:26 (NIV)

Reflect

Faith draws the poison from every grief, takes the sting from every loss, and quenches the fire of every pain; and only faith can do it.

J. G. Holland, writer

Act

Think of ways you can share your blessings with those who are less fortunate.

Pray

Dear Lord, help me to remember that the brightness of Your loving presence is always with me.

Day 214

You will surely forget your trouble, recalling it only as waters gone by.

Job 11:16 (NIV)

Reflect

You are valuable because you exist. Not because of what you do or what you have done, but simply because you are.

Max Lucado, pastor and author

Act

Focus on your blessings, for they are your true worth.

Pray

Dear Lord, help me face life's problems with the sure knowledge that You will always be there.

Day 215

The Spirit of God has made me, and the breath of the Almighty gives me life.

Job 33:4 (ESV)

Reflect

I always like to look on the optimistic side of life, but I am realistic enough to know that life is a complex matter.

Walt Disney

Act

Next time you experience fear, try a "breath prayer." Inhale deeply and pray, "Jesus is with me." Then slowly breath out and pray, "He gives me life."

Pray

Thank You for never leaving my side.

Day 216

Shout for joy, you heavens; rejoice, you earth; burst into song, you mountains! For the LORD comforts his people and will have compassion on his afflicted ones.

Isaiah 49:13 (NIV)

Reflect

Some days there won't be a song in your heart. Sing anyway.

Emory Austin, motivational speaker

Act

Listen to worship music online and sing along as you praise Him and thank Him for your blessings.

Pray

Lord God, help me carry the blessings of prayer into my family's future.

Day 217

Do not boast about tomorrow, for you do not know what a day may bring.

Proverbs 27:1 (NIV)

Reflect

Hope begins in the dark, the stubborn hope that if you just show up and try to do the right thing, the dawn will come. You wait and watch and work: you don't give up.

Anne Lamott, novelist

Act

Every day, affirm that you can make something really good out of your life.

Pray

Heavenly Father, keep my spirit open today to the power of Your guidance and strength.

Day 218

**Blessed are the pure in heart,
for they will see God.**

Matthew 5:8 (NIV)

Reflect

Everything may not be perfect. There are things that may need to change, but you have the grace to be happy today.

Joel Osteen, preacher and author

Act

Remember that circumstances do not make a person—they reveal a person's character.

Pray

Dear Lord, when I place my hope in You, my life is filled in faith and hope.

Day 219

But as for you, be strong and do not give up, for your work will be rewarded.

2 Chronicles 15:7 (NIV)

Reflect

When the dream in our heart is one that God has planted there, a strange happiness flowers into us. At that moment all of the spiritual resources of the universe are released to help us.

Catherine Marshall, author

Act

Lean on Jesus for support when you are enduring trials.

Pray

Heavenly Father, help me learn to love the uncertainties and trials—the works in progress—that You are completing in my life.

Day 220

Commit to the Lord whatever you do, and he will establish your plans.

Proverbs 16:3 (NIV)

Reflect

Believe in yourself! Have faith in your abilities! Without a humble but reasonable confidence in your own powers you cannot be successful or happy.

Norman Vincent Peale, pastor and author

Act

Surrender yourself and your dreams to Jesus and ask Him to work through you.

Pray

Dear Lord, Your goodness is greater than I can imagine. I praise You for Your love, wisdom, forgiveness, and guidance.

Day 221

Whoever dwells in the shelter of the Most High will rest in the shadow of the Almighty.

Psalm 91:1 (NIV)

Reflect

When we put our problems in God's hands, He puts peace in our hearts.

Anonymous

Act

Use the difficulties in your life to increase your ability to love.

Pray

Heavenly Father, I will write this psalm on my heart so that no matter how hard my life may be, I will always be on top of things.

Day 222

The LORD God took the man and put him in the Garden of Eden to work it and take care of it.

Genesis 2:15 (NIV)

Reflect

True happiness is not attained through self-gratification, but through fidelity to a worthy purpose.

Helen Keller

Act

Realize that your job is an essential part of your spiritual growth.

Pray

Dear Lord, You have put miraculous work into each one of us. Help me live my life so that it meets Your plans.

Day 223

I consider that our present sufferings are not worth comparing with the glory that will be revealed in us.

Romans 8:18 (NIV)

Reflect

The natural flights of the human mind are not from pleasure to pleasure, but from hope to hope.

Samuel Johnson, poet and writer

Act

Share with a friend how God is working in your life and encouraging you on your journey.

Pray

Lord, fill me with hope.

Day 224

Ah, Sovereign LORD, you have made the heavens and the earth by your great power and outstretched arm. Nothing is too hard for you.

Jeremiah 32:17 (NIV)

Reflect

It is impossible for that man to despair who remembers that his Helper is omnipotent.

Jeremy Taylor, author

Act

Turn to God in prayer and ask for help to overcome your doubt.

Pray

Lord, thank You for the many ways in which I may lift my heart and spirit through prayer.

Day 225

For this is the will of God, that by doing good you should put to silence the ignorance of foolish people.

1 Peter 2:15 (ESV)

Reflect

God has editing rights over our prayers. He will edit them, correct them, bring them in line with His will and then hand them back to us to be resubmitted.

Stephen Crotts, pastor

Act

Sit with a friend in need and just listen.

Pray

Father, guide me to say and do the right things.

Day 226

In return for my friendship they accuse me, but I am a man of prayer.

Psalm 109:4 (NIV)

Reflect

Prayer—secret, fervent, believing prayer—lies at the root of all personal godliness.

William Carey, missionary

Act

Pray for God to help you keep your focus on Him and off your problems.

Pray

Lord, thank You for the many ways in which I may lift my heart and spirit through prayer.

Day 227

And not only that, but we also glory in tribulations, knowing that tribulation produces perseverance; and perseverance, character; and character, hope.

Romans 5:3–4 (NKJV)

Reflect

If you want to lift yourself up, lift up someone else.

Booker T. Washington, educator and author

Act

Relax and think enthusiastic and positive thoughts about yourself.

Pray

Lord, give me the determination to reach goals I didn't know I had.

Day 228

Call upon Me in the day of trouble; I will deliver you, and you shall glorify Me.

Psalm 50:15 (NKVJ)

Reflect

Prayer may not change things for you,
but it for sure changes you for things.

Samuel Shoemaker, priest

Act

When you feel stuck, take a deep breath and ask God to calm your troubled heart.

Pray

Remember that no matter how overwhelming your problems, you have no reason to fear. God will help you.

Day 229

For we are God's handiwork, created in Christ Jesus to do good works, which God prepared in advance for us to do.

Ephesians 2:10 (NIV)

Reflect

God never hurries. There are no deadlines against which He must work. Only to know this is to quiet our spirits and relax our nerves.

A. W. Tozer, pastor and author

Act

Relax and accept God's grace in times of stress.

Pray

Lord, slow me down. Help me to feel the sun upon my face.

Day 230

May the Lord direct your hearts into God's love and Christ's perseverance.

2 Thessalonians 3:5 (NIV)

Reflect

Promise me you'll always remember: You're braver than you believe, stronger than you seem, and smarter than you think.

A. A. Milne, writer

Act

As you eat breakfast, pray for courage as you thank Him for your daily bread.

Pray

Dear Lord, give me the courage to face anything.

Day 231

Obey them not only to win their favor when their eye is on you, but as slaves of Christ, doing the will of God from your heart.

Ephesians 6:6 (NIV)

Reflect

All labor that uplifts humanity has dignity and importance and should be undertaken with painstaking excellence.

Martin Luther King, Jr.

Act

Grasp every opportunity to offer encouragement to others.

Pray

Lord, let my words and actions seek to uplift another whose load may need lightening and brightening today.

Day 232

Sacrifice thank offerings to God, fulfill your vows to the Most High, and call on me in the day of trouble; I will deliver you, and you will honor me.

Psalm 50:14–15 (NIV)

Reflect

Happiness depends on happenings;
joy depends on Christ.

Anonymous

Act

Surround yourself with others who support your relationship with God.

Pray

Lord, when I fall off track, help guide me back in the direction You have for me.

Day 233

Let us therefore make every effort to do what leads to peace and to mutual edification.

Romans 14:19 (NIV)

Reflect

Maybe that's why life is so precious. No rewind or fast forward...just patience and faith.

Cristina Marrero, author and blogger

Act

Take a moment, close your eyes, and feel God's abundant love.

Pray

Lord, keep me faithful in serving You all the days of my life.

Day 234

Not that we Lord it over your faith, but we work with you for your joy, because it is by faith you stand firm.

2 Corinthians 1:24 (NIV)

Reflect

When one door of happiness closes, another opens, but often we look so long at the closed door that we do not see the one that has been opened for us.

Helen Keller

Act

Make today the day you share love and understanding with your children, giving them the happiness that families are meant to know.

Pray

God, help me to see the good in others and to be as generous as You are.

Day 235

Submit yourselves, then, to God. Resist the devil, and he will flee from you.

James 4:7 (NIV)

Reflect

The Bible is God's chart for you to steer by, to keep you from the bottom of the sea, and to show you where the harbor is, and how to reach it without running on rocks or bars.

Henry Ward Beecher, clergyman

Act

Let God speak to you through His Word.

Pray

Father, our steady Guide, be present with us, pointing out the way You want us to go.

Day 236

You are my refuge and my shield; I have put my hope in your word.

Psalm 119:114 (NIV)

Reflect

I may never know the answers to the questions that plagued me after 9/11. But I know if we lean on God and each other we will be guided to a better, brighter future.

Michael Hingson, 9/11 survivor

Act

Pray for the families and friends of those who have lost their lives.

Pray

Dear Lord, comfort and heal those who are grieving.

Day 237

Blessed is the one who reads aloud the words of this prophecy, and blessed are those who hear it and take to heart what is written in it, because the time is near.

Revelation 1:3 (NIV)

Reflect

Our sense of joy, satisfaction, and fulfillment in life increases, no matter what the circumstances, if we are in the center of God's will.

Billy Graham

Act

Do you want to be able to trust God's way? Pray for wisdom. Pray for the desire and power to follow His will.

Pray

Heavenly Father, there is no joy like the joy of knowing that I'm walking in Your plan for my life.

Day 238

And I will ask the Father, and he will give you another Helper, to be with you forever.

John 14:16 (ESV)

Reflect

God shields us from most of the things we fear, but when He chooses not to shield us, He unfailingly allots grace in the measure needed.

Elisabeth Elliot, author

Act

Reach out to a trusted friend for comfort and strength.

Pray

Dear God, thank You for friends who support me in my time of need.

Day 239

But I trust in you, Lord; I say, "You are my God."

Psalm 31:14 (NIV)

Reflect

Have a sincere desire to serve God and mankind, and stop doubting, stop thinking negatively. Simply start living by faith, pray earnestly and humbly, and get into the habit of looking expectantly for the best.

Norman Vincent Peale, pastor and author

Act

Dedicate your life to becoming like God, understanding that everything that happens to you has spiritual significance.

Pray

Nothing is too hard for me, Lord, as long as it takes me back to You.

Day 240

Through him all things were made; without him nothing was made that has been made.

John 1:3 (NIV)

Reflect

The greater your knowledge of the goodness and grace of God on your life, the more likely you are to praise Him in the storm.

Matt Chandler, pastor

Act

Take a moment to thank Him for His continued work in your life.

Pray

Dear Lord, today I will notice Your hand in the details that magnify Your love here on earth.

Day 241

All people are like grass, and all their glory is like the flowers of the field; the grass withers and the flowers fall, but the word of the Lord endures forever.

1 Peter 1:24–25 (NIV)

Reflect

God meets daily needs daily. Not weekly or annually. He will give you what you need when it is needed.

Max Lucado, pastor and author

Act

Trust that there is a divine plan.

Pray

Thank You, Lord, that You know our needs and are always ready to meet them.

Day 242

You are the LORD, you alone. You have made heaven, the heaven of heavens, with all their host, the earth and all that is on it, the seas and all that is in them; and you preserve all of them; and the host of heaven worships you.

Nehemiah 9:6 (ESV)

Reflect

Never lose an opportunity of seeing anything beautiful, for beauty is God's handwriting.

Ralph Waldo Emerson

Act

Look around you today and thank God for His creation.

Pray

Lord, as the seasons and days change, help us hold fast to Your bright love.

Day 243

Therefore, I urge you, brothers and sisters, in view of God's mercy, to offer your bodies as a living sacrifice, holy and pleasing to God—this is your true and proper worship.

Romans 12:1 (NIV)

Reflect

When wealth is lost, nothing is lost; when health is lost, something is lost; when character is lost, all is lost.

Billy Graham

Act

Be a good steward of your whole self and recognize that taking care of yourself is an important aspect of faith.

Pray

Heavenly Father, let my life demonstrate how much You mean to me.

Day 244

But when he saw the wind, he was afraid and, beginning to sink, cried out, "Lord, save me!"

Matthew 14:30 (NIV)

Reflect

Whoever is careless with the truth in small matters cannot be trusted with important matters.

Albert Einstein

Act

When you are in the midst of life's storms, keep your eyes fixed on Jesus.

Pray

Dear God, when I step out of the boat, I trust that You will help me.

Day 245

Oh, how I love your law! I meditate on it all day long.

Psalm 119:97 (NIV)

Reflect

God never puts something in our path where He has not already equipped us to handle.

Dan Ellis, professional hockey player

Act

Recognize that God's instructions are based on His supernatural power which will guide you to carry out His plan for you.

Pray

Heavenly Father, help me follow Your commands.

Day 246

A greedy man stirs up strife, but the one who trusts in the LORD will be enriched.

Proverbs 28:25 (ESV)

Reflect

One of the greatest discoveries a man makes, one of his great surprises, is to find he can do what he was afraid he couldn't do.

Henry Ford, business magnate

Act

Don't focus on your fears or weaknesses. Keep Jesus in mind.

Pray

Dear Lord, thank You for all the opportunities I've had. Help me to be content with the rewards You give.

Day 247

Since we live by the Spirit, let us keep in step with the Spirit.

Galatians 5:25 (NIV)

Reflect

But there is greater comfort in the substance of silence than in the answer to a question.

Thomas Merton, writer and poet

Act

Spend time today talking with Jesus about recent high and low points in your life.

Pray

Creator God, thank You for the works of Your hand that cry out the awesome truth of Your care for me.

Day 248

He will not fear bad news; His heart is steadfast, trusting in the Lord.

Psalm 112:7 (NASB)

Reflect

Prayer pushes us through life's slumps, propels us over the humps, and pulls us out of the dumps. Prayer is the oomph we need to get the answers we seek.

Max Lucado, pastor and author

Act

Trust that things will be fine.

Pray

God in heaven, hear my prayers and lead me on a never-ending journey to know You better.

Day 249

Do not work for the food that perishes, but for the food that endures to eternal life, which the Son of Man will give to you. For on him God the Father has set his seal.

John 6:27 (ESV)

Reflect

God is speaking to all of us, all the time.
The question is not, to whom does God talk?
The question is, who listens?

Neale Donald Walsch, author

Act

Ask God to stay with you in difficult situations.
Affirm that He is helping you now.

Pray

Dear God, lead me through today with
new insights and new hope.

Day 250

Your eyes will see the king in his beauty and view a land that stretches afar.

Isaiah 33:17 (NIV)

Reflect

The highest form of worship is the worship of unselfish Christian service. The greatest form of praise is the sound of consecrated feet seeking out the lost and helpless.

Billy Graham

Act

Take your beliefs seriously, honoring them in your actions.

Pray

Lord, may all that I do be praise for Your glory.

Day 251

Look at the birds of the air; they do not sow or reap or store away in barns, and yet your heavenly Father feeds them. Are you not much more valuable than they?

Matthew 6:26 (NIV)

Reflect

God says we don't need to be anxious about anything; we just need to pray about everything.

Stormie Omartian, author

Act

Remember that prayer can work miracles.

Pray

Lord, when I ask You to help, I never have to face any difficulty alone.

Day 252

His master replied, "Well done, good and faithful servant! You have been faithful with a few things; I will put you in charge of many things. Come and share your master's happiness!"

Matthew 25:21 (NIV)

Reflect

Little things seem nothing, but they give peace, like those meadow flowers which individually seem odorless but all together perfume the air.

Georges Bernanos, author

Act

Recognize the importance of the little things.

Pray

Dear Lord, guide me to the little things I can do to please You.

Day 253

Be diligent in these matters; give yourself wholly to them, so that everyone may see your progress.

1 Timothy 4:15 (NIV)

Reflect

Never doubt in the darkness what God has given us in the light.

Francine Rivers, author

Act

Surrender to the moment and recognize every challenge is an opportunity for personal growth.

Pray

Keep me close to You, Lord. Replace my sorrow with the warmth of Your comfort.

Day 254

Likewise, the tongue is a small part of the body, but it makes great boasts. Consider what a great forest is set on fire by a small spark.

James 3:5 (NIV)

Reflect

Friendship is born at the moment one person says to another, "What? You too? I thought I was the only one."

C. S. Lewis, theologian and writer

Act

Use your words to uplift yourself and others.

Pray

Heavenly Father, help me make the world a better place, one word at a time.

Day 255

You will have plenty to eat, until you are full, and you will praise the name of the Lord your God, who has worked wonders for you; never again will my people be shamed.

Joel 2:26 (NIV)

Reflect

Not what we say about our blessings, but how we use them, is the true measure of our thanksgiving.

W. T. Purkiser, preacher and author

Act

Celebrate the unique gifts that you bring to the world.

Pray

Beloved Father, help me share the blessings You have given me.

Day 256

The Lord will fight for you; you need only to be still.

Exodus 14:14 (NIV)

Reflect

Always, everywhere God is present, and always He seeks to discover Himself to each one.

A. W. Tozer, pastor and author

Act

No matter what you are facing, look up and know that God will bring you joy.

Pray

Heavenly Father, thank You for relieving my stress. Because of You I can handle any and all of life's challenges.

Day 257

Judge not, that you be not judged.

Matthew 7:1 (ESV)

Reflect

Read the Bible. Work hard and honestly. And don't complain.

Billy Graham

Act

Start a complaint diet. Cut back and ultimately rid yourself of the unhealthy habit of grumbling.

Pray

Dear Lord, thank You for helping shift my perspective from grumbling to grateful.

Day 258

For we walk by faith, not by sight.

2 Corinthians 5:7 (ESV)

Reflect

Do not strive in your own strength.

Andrew Murray, writer and pastor

Act

Spread seeds of faith by living your life in a way that brings glory to God.

Pray

Father, help me to remember what an amazing gift it is to spend time with You.

Day 259

If you lie down, you will not be afraid; when you lie down, your sleep will be sweet.

Proverbs 3:24 (ESV)

Reflect

We are commanded to stop (literally)... rest, relax, let go, and make time for Him. The scene is one of stillness and quietness, listening and waiting before Him.

Charles R. Swindoll, pastor and author

Act

Take a holiday from your life! Release yourself of your goals and to-do lists.

Pray

Heavenly Father, in times of silence and rest, guide me with Your infinite creativity and wisdom.

Day 260

Knowing this first of all, that no prophecy of Scripture comes from someone's own interpretation. For no prophecy was ever produced by the will of man, but men spoke from God as they were carried along by the Holy Spirit.

2 Peter 1:20–21 (ESV)

Reflect

God never said that the journey would be easy, but He did say that the arrival would be worthwhile.

Max Lucado, pastor and author

Act

Approach life's storms as learning experiences that will help make you a stronger and better person.

Pray

Dear Lord, guide me to being an eager student of life—to see every struggle as a tool to shape me into my best.

Day 261

And this is eternal life, that they know you, the only true God, and Jesus Christ whom you have sent.

John 17:3 (ESV)

Reflect

Prayer is not asking. Prayer is putting oneself in the hands of God, at His disposition, and listening to His voice in the depth of our hearts.

Mother Teresa

Act

Bring divine order into your life by praying on a regular basis.

Pray

Dear God, thank You for the beautiful moments we share—and the miracles You bring to my life when I open my heart to You in prayer.

Day 262

So we continue to preach Christ to each person, using all wisdom to warn and to teach everyone, in order to bring each one into God's presence as a mature person in Christ.

Colossians 1:28 (NCV)

Reflect

The purpose of life is a life of purpose.

Anonymous

Act

Look at a challenging situation from all angles and release your feelings of anger or judgment.

Pray

Heavenly Father, thank You for helping me view the difficult situations in my life from a wider lens.

Day 263

I am with you always, even to the end of the age.

Matthew 28:20 (NASB)

Reflect

God's silence is in no way indicative of His activity or involvement in our lives. He may be silent but He is not still.

Charles Stanley, pastor

Act

Stand up to your fears with faith.

Pray

Thank You, Lord, for the troubled times that strengthen our souls and help us grow.

Day 264

I will instruct you and teach you the way you should go.

Psalm 32:8 (NASB)

Reflect

The capacity to care is the thing which gives life its deepest significance.

Pablo Casals, cellist

Act

Remember, love is the only thing okay to do in excess.

Pray

Father, may my gifts to others reflect Your timeless love.

Day 265

There is no fear in love. But perfect love drives out fear, because fear has to do with punishment. The one who fears is not made perfect in love.

1 John 4:18 (NIV)

Reflect

Most of the shadows of this life are caused by our standing in our own sunshine.

Ralph Waldo Emerson

Act

Find strength for today and hope for tomorrow.

Pray

Thank You, Father, for the healing power of hope.

Day 266

The farmer sows the word.

Mark 4:14 (NIV)

Reflect

Nothing is impossible; the word itself says I'm possible!

Audrey Hepburn

Act

Do your best. There is no better achievement than that.

Pray

Father, as I journey forward, set my eyes on all that's good, each day that I live.

Day 267

On the contrary, it is much truer that the members of the body which seem to be weaker are necessary.

1 Corinthians 12:22 (NASB)

Reflect

Humility is not thinking less of yourself, it's thinking of yourself less.

Rick Warren, pastor and author

Act

Open your heart to the kindness of others.

Pray

Dear Father, teach me how to share Your kindness with everyone I meet.

Day 268

And he said unto me, "My grace is sufficient for thee: for my strength is made perfect in weakness."

2 Corinthians 12:9 (KJV)

Reflect

Our prayers lay the track down on which God's power can come.

Watchman Nee, church leader and Christian teacher

Act

Take comfort knowing God is with you.

Pray

Dear God, help me always to see beyond my fears to the beauty of Your creation.

Day 269

Who of you by worrying can add a single hour to your life?

Luke 12:25 (NIV)

Reflect

Live one day without any unhealthy thoughts. It may be difficult, but try another day until it becomes habitual.

Ruth Stafford Peale, writer

Act

Learn to think of opportunity instead of security.

Pray

Lord, light my way along Your path so that all I do leads me toward the destination You have in mind.

Day 270

But you, Lord, do not be far from me. You are my strength; come quickly to help me.

Psalm 22:19 (NIV)

Reflect

Sometimes hope seems as unreal as the angel beside you. But both are there.

Author Unknown

Act

Live with admiration, hope, and love.

Pray

Father, give me goals that stretch my hope to match Your might.

Day 271

The Lord is the strength of his people, a fortress of salvation for his anointed one.

Psalm 28:8 (NIV)

Reflect

Once you become aware that the main business that you are here for is to know God, most of life's problems fall into place of their own accord.

J. I. Packer, Christian theologian

Act

Open your heart and eyes to see that opportunities to help and serve are everywhere.

Pray

Father, help me to do what I can, and in the doing, help me to find new confidence for larger responsibilities.

Day 272

Peter answered Him and said, "Lord, if it is You, command me to come to You on the water."

Matthew 14:28 (NKJV)

Reflect

Success is not final, failure is not fatal: it is the courage to continue that counts.

Winston Churchill

Act

Try something new every day. You never know what you'll end up loving.

Pray

Lord, please give me the courage to take the bold steps required to act.

Day 273

Give me back the joy of your salvation. Keep me strong by giving me a willing spirit.

Psalm 51:12 (NCV)

Reflect

Anxiety is the natural result when our hopes are centered in anything short of God and His will for us.

Billy Graham

Act

When you pray, release your worry and rest in God.

Pray

Dear Lord, help me to persevere in prayer when things seem impossible, knowing that You are the God of possibilities.

Day 274

You shall love your neighbor as yourself.

Matthew 22:39 (NASB)

Reflect

People may refuse our love or reject our message, but they are defenseless against our prayers.

Rick Warren, pastor and author

Act

Perform the little acts that give form and continuity to love.

Pray

Lord, thank You for Your constant love that never changes.

Day 275

Your word is a lamp to my feet and a light to my path.

Psalm 119:105 (NASB)

Reflect

The best one can do when it is raining is let it rain.

Henry Wadsworth Longfellow, poet and educator

Act

Remember that faith will lead you through unsteady times.

Pray

Lord, peace is knowing that Your comfort is only a prayer away.

Day 276

You, LORD, are forgiving and good, abounding in love to all who call to you.

Psalm 86:5 (NIV)

Reflect

Worship is a way of gladly reflecting back to God the radiance of His worth.

John Piper, preacher and author

Act

Pray God's Word and see your prayer life flourish.

Pray

Dear Lord, thank You for listening when I pray, knowing You are never too busy to hear even the smallest request. Help me to remember to come to You with everything.

Day 277

Thanks be to God for his indescribable gift.

2 Corinthians 9:15 (NIV)

Reflect

We ought to see the face of God every morning before we see the face of man.

Dwight L. Moody, evangelist

Act

Welcome the freshness of morning and the opportunities that await you at the start of each new day.

Pray

Lord, help me to welcome each day as a gift from Your hands.

Day 278

Nehemiah said, "Go and enjoy choice food and sweet drinks, and send some to those who have nothing prepared. This day is holy to our Lord. Do not grieve, for the joy of the LORD is your strength."

Nehemiah 8:10 (NIV)

Reflect

Faith is realizing that I am useful to God not in spite of my scars, but because of them.

Pamela Reeve, author

Act

Sit quietly and be sensitive to hear His voice.

Pray

Lord, remind me to cherish the treasures of the world and share them with others.

Day 279

He said to them, "Watch out! Be on your guard against all kinds of greed; life does not consist in an abundance of possessions."

Luke 12:15 (NIV)

Reflect

A state of mind that sees God in everything is evidence of growth in grace and a thankful heart.

Charles G. Finney, minister

Act

Today, be a "hope spreader." Take a cup of coffee to a discouraged coworker, hug your children and tell them how much you love them, or help an elderly neighbor with their overgrown yard.

Pray

Lord, thank You for renewing me and giving me a life that has purpose and meaning.

Day 280

LORD, you alone are my portion and my cup; you make my lot secure. The boundary lines have fallen for me in pleasant places; surely I have a delightful inheritance.

Psalm 16:5–6 (NIV)

Reflect

It is during our darkest moments that we must focus to see the light.

Anonymous

Act

When fear comes, counter it with an affirmation of faith.

Pray

Father, Your love surrounds us; there is no need to fear.

Day 281

If we claim to be without sin, we deceive ourselves and the truth is not in us. If we confess our sins, he is faithful and just and will forgive us our sins and purify us from all unrighteousness.

1 John 1:8–9 (NIV)

Reflect

Start with what is right rather than what is acceptable.

Franz Kafka, novelist

Act

Acknowledge your wrongdoings to Him and ask for forgiveness.

Pray

Dear God, I am sorry for my thoughts and actions; I am ready to receive the amazing blessing of starting anew.

Day 282

I lift up my eyes to the mountains—where does my help come from? My help comes from the Lord, the Maker of heaven and earth. He will not let your foot slip—he who watches over you will not slumber; indeed, he who watches over Israel will neither slumber nor sleep.

Psalm 121:1–4 (NIV)

Reflect

A day of worry is more exhausting than a day of work.

Sir John Lubbock

Act

Start your day with a simple prayer, thanking God for the day.

Pray

Lord, help me to keep my eyes on You today and nothing else.

Day 283

Jesus replied: "Love the Lord your God with all your heart and with all your soul and with all your mind." This is the first and greatest commandment. And the second is like it: "Love your neighbor as yourself."

Matthew 22:37–39 (NIV)

Reflect

While we are waiting on God, we are waiting with God.

Louie Giglio, pastor

Act

Take comfort knowing God is with you.

Pray

Dear God, please let my life be filled with the love Jesus describes.

Day 284

Evening, morning and noon I cry out in distress, and he hears my voice.

Psalm 55:17 (NIV)

Reflect

How you think about a problem is more important than the problem itself. So always think positively.

Norman Vincent Peale, pastor and author

Act

Visualize the protection of being in God's care.

Pray

Dear Lord, grant me the grace to endure the struggle in any area of life where You have placed me.

Day 285

My command is this: Love each other as I have loved you. Greater love has no one than this: to lay down one's life for one's friends.

John 15:12–13 (NIV)

Reflect

To the world you might be one person, but to one person you might be the world.

Source Unknown

Act

Today, be an example of agape love. Be kind, patient, forgiving, and humble.

Pray

You fill me with concern for others, Lord, and You give me strength to help them.

Day 286

**When anxiety was great within me,
your consolation brought me joy.**

Psalm 94:19 (NIV)

Reflect

The art of being happy lies in the power of extracting happiness from common things.

Henry Ward Beecher, clergyman

Act

Make a mental list of happy thoughts and pass them through your mind several times a day.

Pray

Dear Lord, help me to open myself up to the happiness that is mine today.

Day 287

The Lord gives strength to his people; the Lord blesses his people with peace.

Psalm 29:11 (NIV)

Reflect

If you don't like something, change it; if you can't change it, change the way you think about it.

Mary Engelbreit, artist

Act

Remember that sometimes the smallest gesture can change the world.

Pray

Lord, I must remember that Your world is ever-changing, but You are constant.

Day 288

My flesh and my heart may fail, but God is the strength of my heart and my portion forever.

Psalm 73:26 (NIV)

Reflect

When I have learnt to love God better than my earthly dearest, I shall love my earthly dearest better than I do now.

C. S. Lewis, theologian and writer

Act

Remember, love is the only thing okay to do in excess.

Pray

Keep me open to Your great love.

Day 289

But now even more the report about him went abroad, and great crowds gathered to hear him and to be healed of their infirmities. But he would withdraw to desolate places and pray.

Luke 5:15–16 (ESV)

Reflect

Worry is the darkroom in which negatives can develop.

Wanda E. Brunstetter, author

Act

Lay your burdens at His feet, knowing that quiet time and trust enhance your awareness of His presence.

Pray

Heavenly Father, help me remember that I don't need to handle everything on my own.

Day 290

One of them, when he saw he was healed, came back, praising God in a loud voice. He threw himself at Jesus's feet and thanked him—and he was a Samaritan.

Luke 17:15–16 (NIV)

Reflect

When one has a grateful heart, life is so beautiful.

Roy T. Bennett

Act

Be thankful in Him, because He is our constant, stable Source of strength and comfort.

Pray

Lord Jesus, because of You I am learning to be thankful for every single breath.

Day 291

He has shown you, O mortal, what is good. And what does the LORD require of you? To act justly and to love mercy and to walk humbly with your God.

Micah 6:8 (NIV)

Reflect

Blessings can come in a number of ways.
The Lord doesn't give you what you want;
the Lord gives you what you need.

Eric Davis, former professional baseball player

Act

Find, in every hour, some heavenly blessings.

Pray

Father, help us to live joyously, to celebrate the song in our heart, and to rejoice always.

Day 292

Though he may stumble, he will not fall, for the LORD upholds him with his hand. I was young and now I am old, yet I have never seen the righteous forsaken or their children begging bread.

Psalm 37:24–25 (NIV)

Reflect

Meet your fears with faith.

Max Lucado, pastor and author

Act

When you are full of fear, confused, out of control, filled with doubt, or so busy you can barely see straight, know He is there to guide you.

Pray

Lord Jesus, I am so grateful that You are with me, holding me in the palm of Your hand.

Day 293

All Scripture is God-breathed and is useful for teaching, rebuking, correcting and training in righteousness.

2 Timothy 3:16 (NIV)

Reflect

To one who has faith, no explanation is necessary. To one without faith, no explanation is possible.

Thomas Aquinas, priest

Act

Ask God to restore your spirit and improve your outlook.

Pray

Lord, give me strength to face what once seemed overwhelming.

Day 294

Again, truly I tell you that if two of you on earth agree about anything they ask for, it will be done for them by my Father in heaven.

Matthew 18:19 (NIV)

Reflect

This should be the motto for every follower of Jesus Christ: Never stop praying, no matter how dark and hopeless it may seem.

Billy Graham

Act

When faced with darkness, turn to the light of God.

Pray

Lord, peace is knowing that Your comfort is only a prayer away.

Day 295

In all your ways acknowledge him, and he will make straight your paths.

Proverbs 3:6 (ESV)

Reflect

Faith is like radar that sees through the fog.

Corrie ten Boom, writer

Act

Find strength for today and hope for tomorrow.

Pray

Dear Lord, help me face life's problems with the sure knowledge that You'll always be there.

Day 296

Many are the plans in a person's heart, but it is the LORD's purpose that prevails.

Proverbs 19:21 (NIV)

Reflect

Feed your faith and your doubts will starve to death.

Debbie Macomber, author

Act

Relinquish your sense of control and be flexible. Trust God's plan is at work.

Pray

Heavenly Father, help me to graciously accept changes knowing that in a world of unknowns and twists and turns You are constant.

Day 297

He has sent Me to heal the brokenhearted.

Luke 4:18 (NKJV)

Reflect

Sorrow is a fruit. God does not make it grow on limbs too weak to bear it.

Victor Hugo, writer and politician

Act

Ask Jesus to mend your broken heart during times of sorrow and sadness.

Pray

When grief strikes, help me draw strength from Your great love.

Day 298

Today, if only you would hear his voice, "Do not harden your hearts as you did at Meribah, as you did that day at Massah in the wilderness."

Psalm 95:8 (NIV)

Reflect

We savor these moments, when we are conscious of love's presence, these holy moments of gratitude. And that is grace.

Anne Lamott, writer

Act

Praise Him for being able to redeem every situation and for converting your challenges into positive growth.

Pray

Heavenly Father, thank You for giving me so many reasons to praise You.

Day 299

Out of his fullness we have all received grace in place of grace already given.

John 1:16 (NIV)

Reflect

Your worst days are never so bad that you are beyond the reach of God's grace. And your best days are never so good that you are beyond the need of God's grace.

Jerry Bridges, author and speaker

Act

Repeat the above Scripture and imagine His grace flowing upon you and filling you with divine light.

Pray

Heavenly Father, each day in my life is a sacred gift from You, designed by You and filled with grace upon grace.

Day 300

No one has seen the Father except the one who is from God; only he has seen the Father.

John 6:46 (NIV)

Reflect

We may speak about a place where there are no tears, no death, no fear, no night; but those are just the benefits of heaven. The beauty of heaven is seeing God.

Max Lucado, pastor and author

Act

Trust that God understands your situation. He has all the answers.

Pray

God, help me to recognize Your influence in my life.

Day 301

Because he himself suffered when he was tempted, he is able to help those who are being tempted.

Hebrews 2:18 (NIV)

Reflect

Of all the liars in the world, sometimes the worst are your own fears.

Rudyard Kipling, writer

Act

Bring your suffering to Him in prayer. He feels Your pain as you feel His comfort.

Pray

Heavenly Father, on days when I feel tested, I know I can go on because You are with me.

Day 302

But thanks be to God! He gives us the victory through our Lord Jesus Christ.

1 Corinthians 15:57 (NIV)

Reflect

When a person doesn't have gratitude, something is missing in his or her humanity.

Elie Wiesel, writer

Act

Make right now your focus. Appreciate where you are and be grateful that you are here.

Pray

Teach me to be thankful at all times, Lord.

Day 303

The seed that fell among the thorns represents others who hear God's word, but all too quickly the message is crowded out by the worries of this life, the lure of wealth, and the desire for other things, so no fruit is produced.

Mark 4:18–19 (NLT)

Reflect

With arms outstretched I thank. With heart beating gratefully I love. With body in health I jump for joy. With spirit full I love.

Terri Guillemets, quotation anthologist

Act

Every day is the perfect time to thank God for giving us a fruitful life.

Pray

Heavenly Father, thank You for helping me weed unhealthy worries and thoughts from my life.

Day 304

The Son radiates God's own glory and expresses the very character of God, and he sustains everything by the mighty power of his command. When he had cleansed us from our sins, he sat down in the place of honor at the right hand of the majestic God in heaven.

Hebrews 1:3 (NLT)

Reflect

Imperfection is the prerequisite for grace. Light only gets in through the cracks.

Philip Yancey, author

Act

As the day draws to a close, know that God's glory is all around you. Even on dark days when the news is bleak or family troubles rise to a hilt, focus on His love for you.

Pray

Lord Jesus, thank You for bringing unexpected light to dark days.

Day 305

Therefore, there is now no condemnation for those who are in Christ Jesus, because through Christ Jesus the law of the Spirit who gives life has set you free from the law of sin and death.

Romans 8:1–2 (NIV)

Reflect

Every burden prepares you for eternity.

Basilea Schlink, religious leader and writer

Act

Pray for Jesus to help you let go of any burdens—what-ifs or should haves that weigh on your mind.

Pray

Heavenly Father, help me release my hurts and shame; help me break free.

Day 306

If you, O Lord, should mark iniquities, O Lord, who could stand? But with you there is forgiveness, that you may be feared.

Psalm 130:3–4 (ESV)

Reflect

Man has two great spiritual needs. One is for forgiveness. The other is for goodness.

Billy Graham

Act

Know that because of Jesus's promise to forgive, no matter how many mistakes we make or problems we create, we can still receive His ever-renewing mercies.

Pray

Lord God, thank You for forgiving me—for lifting guilt from my heart and filling me with Your grace.

Day 307

Is anyone among you in trouble? Let them pray. Is anyone happy? Let them sing songs of praise.

James 5:13 (NIV)

Reflect

A relationship with God is the most important relationship you can have.

Author Unknown

Act

Open your heart to God by training your spirit to recognize and hear His instructions.

Pray

God, I submit the struggles in my life to Your care.

Day 308

For it is God who works in you to will and to act in order to fulfill his good purpose.

Philippians 2:13 (NIV)

Reflect

The hardest arithmetic to master is that which enables us to count our blessings.

Eric Hoffer, philosopher and author

Act

As you read the Bible, be energized through the power and presence of God's Word.

Pray

Heavenly Father, give me the energy to celebrate all the blessings you bestow on me.

Day 309

Enter through the narrow gate. For wide is the gate and broad is the road that leads to destruction, and many enter through it. But small is the gate and narrow the road that leads to life, and only a few find it.

Matthew 7:13–14 (NIV)

Reflect

We ourselves feel that what we are doing is just a drop in the ocean. But the ocean would be less because of that missing drop.

Mother Teresa

Act

Ask Jesus to guide your action and keep you on the less-traveled but more rewarding road that leads to everlasting life.

Prayer

Lord, You are my compass and companion, guiding me to become the best I can be.

Day 310

The engulfing waters threatened me, the deep surrounded me…but you, LORD my God, brought my life up from the pit. When my life was ebbing away, I remembered you.

Jonah 2:5–7 (NIV)

Reflect

Ask for what you want, but be willing to take what God gives you. It may be better than what you asked for.

Norman Vincent Peale, pastor and author

Act

Make a commitment to seek God's presence.

Pray

Heavenly Father, my delight is to be with You. Our time together is a precious gift, a spirit-renewing blessing that grows each day.

Day 311

In the morning sow thy seed, and in the evening withhold not thine hand.

Ecclesiastes 11:6 (KJV)

Reflect

Some people cannot see a good thing when it is right here, right now. Others can sense a good thing coming when it is days, months, or miles away.

Maya Angelou, author and poet

Act

Make a list of five strengths you possess and rejoice in the gifts God has given you.

Pray

Lord, day by day, help me to do what You have designed me to do.

Day 312

LORD, let me speak so I may praise you.

Psalm 51:15 (NCV)

Reflect

The roots of all goodness lie in the soil of appreciation for goodness.

Dalai Lama

Act

Praise God for the gift of today. Reflect on blessings you may be taking for granted.

Pray

Dear Lord, Your goodness is greater than I can imagine. I praise You for Your love, wisdom, forgiveness, and guidance.

Day 313

Why, my soul, are you downcast? Why so disturbed within me? Put your hope in God, for I will yet praise him, my Savior and my God.

Psalm 42:11 (NIV)

Reflect

Faith is believing that God is going to take you places before you even get there.

Matthew Barnett, pastor

Act

Reach out to God and share your deepest thoughts. No matter what is going on in your life, He is with you.

Pray

Lord, I know You are here, beside me, helping me keep my heart and mind lifted above my cares and worries.

Day 314

Bear one another's burdens, and so fulfill the law of Christ.

Galatians 6:2 (ESV)

Reflect

You have not lived today until you have done something for someone who can never repay you.

John Bunyan, writer and preacher

Act

Remember that love shared is multiplied many times over.

Pray

Heavenly Father, guide me to a friend who needs encouragement and prayer.

Day 315

But when the set time had fully come, God sent his Son, born of a woman, born under the law.

Galatians 4:4 (NIV)

Reflect

The only things we can keep are the things we freely give to God.

C. S. Lewis, theologian and writer

Act

Extend your love; share a story; give someone a smile.

Pray

Dear God, through our acts of giving, we lay up treasures in heaven that will last forever.

Day 316

But do not overlook this one fact, beloved, that with the LORD one day is as a thousand years, and a thousand years as one day.

2 Peter 3:8 (ESV)

Reflect

We must cease striving and trust God to provide what He thinks is best and in whatever time He chooses to make it available.

Charles R. Swindoll, pastor and author

Act

Know that nothing is ever too soon or too late that is done in God's time.

Pray

Heavenly Father, when I'm in the midst of waiting, guide me to remember Your timing is always perfect.

Day 317

A new command I give you: Love one another. As I have loved you, so you must love one another.

John 13:34 (NIV)

Reflect

The greatest joys in life are found not only in what we do and feel, but also in our quiet hopes and labors for others.

Bryant McGill, author

Act

Take heart! Recognize that family is one of God's greatest gifts and treasure your time together.

Pray

Dear God, thank You for my family. Shine your love and harmony on us.

Day 318

Owe no one anything, except to love each other, for the one who loves another has fulfilled the law.

Romans 13:8 (ESV)

Reflect

The most obvious lesson in Christ's teaching is that there is no happiness in having or getting anything, but only in giving.

Henry Drummond, author and evangelist

Act

Share with others how important they are to you.

Pray

Dear Lord, help me be a beacon of Your love.

Day 319

Whatever you do, work heartily,
as for the LORD and not for men.

Colossians 3:23 (ESV)

Reflect

Love is the immortal flow of energy that nourishes, extends, and preserves. Its eternal goal is life.

Smiley Blanton, psychiatrist

Act

Turn to the Source of all energy—God!

Pray

Heavenly Father, refresh my spirit. Give me the strength and enthusiasm to get ready for each new day.

Day 320

**And now, Lord, for what do I wait?
My hope is in You.**

Psalm 39:7 (NASB)

Reflect

Hope is being able to see that there is light despite all of the darkness.

Desmond Tutu

Act

Spend time with God, thanking Him for all He has done for you.

Pray

Fill my heart with Your love, dear Lord, and guide me with Your wisdom.

Day 321

Discretion will watch over you,
understanding will guard you.

Proverbs 3:11 (NASB)

Reflect

We spend precious hours fearing the inevitable. It would be wise to use that time adoring our families, cherishing our friends, and living our lives.

Maya Angelou, author and poet

Act

Look to Him for guidance and be thankful that He will correct your ways when you slip off His path.

Pray

Heavenly Father, help me continue to grow. Lead me to be my best today and every day.

Day 322

"For my thoughts are not your thoughts,
neither are your ways my ways,"
declares the Lord.

Isaiah 55:8 (NIV)

Reflect

We need to give each other the space to grow, to be ourselves, to exercise our diversity. We need to give each other space so that we may both give and receive such beautiful things as ideas, openness, dignity, joy, healing, and inclusion.

Max de Pree, businessman

Act

Give your joy to others and it will come back to you.

Pray

Father, fulfill Your purposes for me and help me to give myself generously to others without reservation.

Day 323

He says to the snow, "Fall on the earth," and to the shower, "Be a heavy rain."

Job 37:6 (NCV)

Reflect

The only limits to the possibilities in your life tomorrow are the buts you use today.

Les Brown, politician and motivational speaker

Act

Reflect on God's greatness that goes beyond what He has created. Nothing is beyond His power.

Pray

Father, Your unfailing love is as high as the heavens. Your faithfulness reaches to the clouds. May Your glory shine over all the earth.

Day 324

For no matter how many promises God has made, they are "Yes" in Christ. And so through him the "Amen" is spoken by us to the glory of God.

2 Corinthians 1:20 (NIV)

Reflect

Our Lord has written the promise of resurrection, not in books alone, but in every leaf in springtime.

Martin Luther, priest

Act

Study Scripture and recognize His promises are always yes.

Prayer

Lord, thank You for hearing and answering my prayers.

Day 325

Each of you should use whatever gift you have received to serve others, as faithful stewards of God's grace in its various forms.

1 Peter 4:10 (NIV)

Reflect

Truth is a deep kindness that teaches us to be content in our everyday life and share with the people the same happiness.

Khalil Gibran, writer, poet, and visual artist

Act

Share with others the gifts of grace God has given you.

Pray

Lord, guide me to give my time, love, and energy, so others may know the gift of Your presence.

Day 326

You intended to harm me, but God intended it for good to accomplish what is now being done, the saving of many lives.

Genesis 50:20 (NIV)

Reflect

May the perfect grace and eternal love of Christ our Lord be our never-failing protection and help.

Saint Ignatius

Act

Leave everything in God's hands and you will see God's hands in everything.

Pray

Heavenly Father, guide me to release any worries that entangle my heart so I may joyfully follow the path You have prepared for me.

Day 327

While you were doing all these things, declares the Lord, I spoke to you again and again, but you did not listen; I call you, but you did not answer.

Jeremiah 7:13 (NIV)

Reflect

We have two ears and one mouth so that we can listen twice as much as we speak.

Epictetus, philosopher

Act

Quiet your mind to receive God's messages.

Pray

Lord, help me to seek Your voice and hear Your promises and plans for me.

Day 328

Be kind and compassionate to one another, forgiving each other, just as in Christ God forgave you.

Ephesians 4:32 (NIV)

Reflect

We are more alike, my friends, than we are unalike.

Maya Angelou, author and poet

Act

Ask God to heal your heart so you can move forward on life's journey without the burdens of the past weighing on you.

Pray

Father, help me to release the hurt so I can love with my whole heart and forgive as freely as You forgive.

Day 329

For the Mighty One has done great things for me—holy is his name.

Luke 1:49 (NIV)

Reflect

Human greatness does not lie in wealth or power, but in character and goodness. People are just people, and all people have faults and shortcomings, but all of us are born with a basic goodness.

Anne Frank

Act

Let God fill you with His Spirit as He empowers you to walk in truth.

Pray

Mighty One, I praise You. Holy is Your name.

Day 330

Fear not, for I have redeemed you; I have called you by name, you are mine.

Isaiah 43:1 (ESV)

Reflect

I'm convinced of this: Good done anywhere is good done everywhere. For a change, start by speaking to people rather than walking by them like they're stones that don't matter. As long as you're breathing, it's never too late to do some good.

Maya Angelou, author and poet

Act

Take His Word deep into your heart as if it is meant specifically for you—because it is!

Pray

Lord God, You have called me by name, and I am here to serve You.

Day 331

I will walk in freedom, for I have devoted myself to your commandments.

Psalm 119:45 (NLT)

Reflect

All the great things are simple, and many can be expressed in a single word: freedom, justice, honor, duty, mercy, hope.

Winston Churchill

Act

Ask God to help you embrace and honor His commands.

Pray

Thank You, Lord, for being the key to my freedom.

Day 332

May he give you the desire of your heart and make all your plans succeed.

Psalm 20:4 (NIV)

Reflect

The price of success is hard work, dedication to the job at hand, and the determination that whether we win or lose, we have applied the best of ourselves to the task at hand.

Vince Lombardi, football coach

Act

Ask God to help you take the necessary steps to achieve your goals.

Pray

Father, help me clearly define what I want to do. Guide me to make every day count.

Day 333

Because of the Lord's great love we are not consumed, for his compassions never fail. They are new every morning; great is your faithfulness.

Lamentations 3:22–23 (NIV)

Reflect

Sometimes all it takes is a subtle shift in perspective, an opening of the mind, an intentional pause and reset, or a new route to start to see new options and new possibilities.

Kristin Armstrong, professional cyclist

Act

Listen for God's urgings to see new possibilities.

Pray

Dear Lord, help me to see the new life that can be mine just by carving a new path.

Day 334

For in the same way you judge others, you will be judged, and with the measure you use, it will be measured to you.

Matthew 7:2 (NIV)

Reflect

At the Day of Judgment, we shall not be asked what we have read, but what we have done.

Thomas a Kempis, canon and author

Act

Work on improving yourself by being more accepting, less anxious, and more cheerful!

Pray

Lord, guide me to place my focus and efforts on improving myself.

Day 335

No, I tell you, but unless you change your hearts and lives, you will die just as they did.

Luke 13:3 (CEB)

Reflect

Change your opinions, keep to your principles; change your leaves, keep intact your roots.

Victor Hugo, writer and politician

Act

Search your heart and surrender any habits, feelings, thoughts, and actions that need to be transformed for you to be closer to God.

Pray

Loving Father, help me change my heart so I live my life so that it pleases You.

Day 336

**Sing to the LORD, praise his name;
proclaim his salvation day after day.**

Psalm 96:2 (NIV)

Reflect

Where words fail, music speaks.

Hans Christian Anderson, author

Act

Turn on your favorite playlist and sing along, knowing your voice is heard by God.

Pray

Lord, today I sing to You!

Day 337

Now finish the work, so that your eager willingness to do it may be matched by your completion of it, according to your means.

2 Corinthians 8:11 (NIV)

Reflect

Strength does not come from physical capacity. It comes from an indomitable will.

Mahatma Gandhi

Act

Be patient in your work, knowing Jesus has promised you power and strength to finish the work He has planned for you.

Pray

Lord, help me to boldly serve You.

Day 338

Make this tabernacle and all its furnishings exactly like the pattern I will show you.

Exodus 25:9 (NIV)

Reflect

Great things are done by a series of small things brought together.

Vincent Van Gogh

Act

Today, share with God everything that is on your mind, even the smallest things.

Pray

Dear God, thank You for working out every detail for the good in my life.

Day 339

We have this as a sure and steadfast anchor of the soul, a hope that enters into the inner place behind the curtain.

Hebrews 6:19 (ESV)

Reflect

Cast your cares on God; that anchor holds.

Frank Moore Colby, educator and writer

Act

Allow God's presence to shed His light on whatever is troubling your heart.

Pray

Lord, thank You for being my anchor, steadfast and strong, upholding me and steadying my spirit.

Day 340

If you go the wrong way—to the right or to the left—you will hear a voice behind you saying, "This is the right way. You should go this way."

Isaiah 30:21 (NCV)

Reflect

I'm always feeling like I'm lacking wisdom. This reassurance that one can ask God for that and it will happen is certainly reassuring to me.

Francis Collins, physician

Act

Make it part of your prayer practice to check in with Jesus and ask for reassurance that you are on track.

Pray

Lord, guide me on this journey of life.

Day 341

Watch and pray, lest you enter into temptation. The spirit indeed is willing, but the flesh is weak.

Mark 14:38 (NKJV)

Reflect

Darkness comes. In the middle of it, the future looks blank. The temptation to quit is huge. Don't. You are in good company... You will argue with yourself that there is no way forward. But with God, nothing is impossible. He has more ropes and ladders and tunnels out of pits than you can conceive. Wait. Pray without ceasing. Hope.

John Piper, theologian

Act

Ask Jesus for the wisdom to walk away when you need to.

Pray

Lord, You have prepared the perfect way for me to ward off temptation. Fill me with Your strength.

Day 342

**Hear me, Lord, and answer me,
for I am poor and needy.**

Psalm 86:1 (NIV)

Reflect

The ultimate measure of a man is not where he stands in moments of comfort and convenience, but where he stands at times of challenge and controversy.

Martin Luther King, Jr.

Act

Reach out to God and tell Him that He is your true Source of comfort.

Pray

Lord, I am poor and needy. Please be with me.

Day 343

From the ends of the earth I call to you, I call as my heart grows faint; lead me to the rock that is higher than I.

Psalm 61:2 (NIV)

Reflect

Character cannot be developed in ease and quiet. Only through experience of trial and suffering can the soul be strengthened, ambition inspired, and success achieved.

Helen Keller

Act

When you are distressed, call out to God, the Rock of Salvation, to bring you comfort and stability.

Pray

Father, when my heart grows faint, lead me to You—my Rock—that is higher than I.

Day 344

You have granted me life and favor, and Your care has preserved my spirit.

Job 10:12 (NKJV)

Reflect

Through hard work, perseverance, and a faith in God, you can live your dreams.

Ben Carson, surgeon and politician

Act

Seek God's face every day, trusting that He shines goodness on you.

Pray

Keep me facing forward, God.

Day 345

For great is your love, reaching to the heavens; your faithfulness reaches to the skies.

Psalm 57:10 (NIV)

Reflect

In my deepest, darkest moments, what really got me through was a prayer. Sometimes my prayer was "Help me." Sometimes a prayer was "Thank you." What I've discovered is that intimate connection and communication with my creator will always get me through because I know my support, my help, is just a prayer away.

Iyanla Vanzant, inspirational speaker

Act

Build up your spirit, day by day, with the power of God's presence in your life and His eternal love for you.

Pray

Lord, I praise You for Your faithfulness!

Day 346

On the contrary, we speak as those approved by God to be entrusted with the Gospel. We are not trying to please people but God, who tests our hearts.

1 Thessalonians 2:4 (NIV)

Reflect

If you talk to a man in a language he understands, that goes to his head. If you talk to him in his language, that goes to his heart.

Nelson Mandela

Act

Spend quiet time with God, asking Him to guide you in living your life in a way that honors Him.

Pray

Almighty God, You are the center of my life. I trust You with my decisions.

Day 347

And a highway will be there; it will be called the Way of Holiness; it will be for those who walk on that Way. The unclean will not journey on it; wicked fools will not go about on it.

Isaiah 35:8 (NIV)

Reflect

The joy of life comes from our encounters with new experiences, and hence there is no greater joy than to have an endlessly changing horizon, for each day to have a new and different sun.

Christopher McCandless, adventurer

Act

Take a moment and praise God for the positive changes happening in your faith and in your life.

Pray

Lord, keep me moving forward spiritually. Help keep me on the path to holiness.

Day 348

A person's wisdom yields patience; it is to one's glory to overlook an offense.

Proverbs 19:11 (NIV)

Reflect

Patience is not simply the ability to wait—it's how we behave while we're waiting.

Joyce Meyer, author

Act

The next time you feel your temper rising, take a deep breath and rise above provocation.

Pray

Lord, help me to keep control of my emotions so that I react to upsetting situations with patience and understanding.

Day 349

Do not neglect your gift…

1 Timothy 4:14 (NIV)

Reflect

You are never too old to set another goal or to dream a new dream.

Les Brown, politician and motivational speaker

Act

Look deep in your heart to see if there is an unfulfilled goal you have given up on, despite gentle nudges from above. Press onward.

Pray

Gracious God, thank You for instilling desires in me that sometimes seem out of reach.

Day 350

I keep asking that God of our LORD Jesus Christ, the glorious Father, may give you the Spirit of wisdom and revelation, so that you may know him better.

Ephesians 1:17 (NIV)

Reflect

If you realized how powerful your thoughts are, you would never think a negative thought.

Peace Pilgrim, spiritual teacher

Act

Ask God to open your heart—to unveil the power and beauty of who He is.

Pray

God, help me to feel Your presence and to experience Your power.

Day 351

What do you think? If a man owns a hundred sheep, and one of them wanders away, will he not leave the ninety-nine on the hills and go to look for the one that wandered off?

Matthew 18:12 (NIV)

Reflect

Christ's flock is made up of sheep that not only listen to their shepherd, but are also able to recognize his voice, to follow him, faithfully and with full awareness, on the pastures of eternal life.

Pope John XXIII

Act

Thank God for going to any length to find you when you go astray and bring you home.

Pray

Help me to remember, Father, how much You love me.

Day 352

A gentle answer turns away wrath, but a harsh word stirs up anger.

Proverbs 15:1 (NIV)

Reflect

Never be in a hurry; do everything quietly and in a calm spirit. Do not lose your inner peace for anything whatsoever, even if your whole world seems upset.

Saint Francis de Sales

Act

When you face conflict, ask for God's strength to stay calm and to see the situation from all perspectives.

Pray

Heavenly Father, help me to be the voice of peace.

Day 353

Then a voice came from heaven, "You are My beloved Son, in whom I am well pleased."

Mark 1:11 (NKJV)

Reflect

The art of acceptance is the art of making someone who has just done you a small favor wish that he might have done you a greater one.

Martin Luther King, Jr.

Act

Spend a few minutes laughing with the Lord today—let Him enjoy your company.

Pray

God, thank You for loving me just the way I am.

Day 354

I remain confident of this: I will see the goodness of the LORD in the land of the living.

Psalm 27:13 (NIV)

Reflect

God's dream is that you and I and all of us will realize that we are family, that we are made for togetherness, for goodness, and for compassion.

Desmond Tutu

Act

Start a joy journal and log God's goodness daily.

Pray

Lord, thank You for helping me look for goodness in others.

Day 355

Precisely because they have misled my people, saying, "Peace," when there is no peace...

Ezekiel 13:10 (ESV)

Reflect

But if you possess faith, your heart cannot do otherwise than laugh for joy in God, and grow free, confident, and courageous. For how can the heart remain sorrowful and dejected when it entertains no doubt of God's kindness to it, and of his attitude as a good friend with whom it may unreservedly and freely enjoy all things?

Martin Luther, priest

Act

Today, show someone a glimpse of Jesus in you.

Pray

Jesus, even when life is hard, help me to keep joy vibrant and visible to others.

Day 356

Be perfect, therefore, as your heavenly Father is perfect.

Matthew 5:48 (NIV)

Reflect

Find ecstasy in life; the mere sense of living is joy enough.

Emily Dickinson, poet

Act

Take a moment to remember that God has blessed you with unique gifts and talents.

Pray

Lord, when I am hard on myself, guide me back to the beautiful truth that I am right where I am supposed to be.

Day 357

He said, Go and tell this people: "Be ever hearing, but never understanding; be ever seeing, but never perceiving."

Isaiah 6:9 (NIV)

Reflect

Forgiveness is an act of the will, and the will can function regardless of the temperature of the heart.

Corrie ten Boom, writer

Act

Next time you have feelings of resentment or shame, ask God for His forgiveness.

Pray

Thank You, Father, for Your compassion and for reminding me that as Your child, I am worthy of Your love and forgiveness.

Day 358

Love the Lord your God with all your heart and with all your soul and with all your mind and with all your strength.

Mark 12:30 (NIV)

Reflect

What we have once enjoyed we can never lose. All that we love deeply becomes a part of us.

Helen Keller

Act

Take a moment and feel your heart swell with love, and thank Him for the magnificent process of getting to know Him.

Pray

Lord, I am overflowing with thankfulness that You are with me.

Day 359

But when you ask, you must believe and not doubt, because the one who doubts is like a wave of the sea, blown and tossed by the wind. That person should not expect to receive anything from the Lord.

James 1:6–7 (NIV)

Reflect

Our heavenly Father understands our disappointment, suffering, pain, fear, and doubt. He is always there to encourage our hearts and help us understand that He's sufficient for all of our needs. When I accepted this as an absolute truth in my life, I found that my worrying stopped.

Charles Stanley, pastor

Act

Do you feel like you're in a season of waiting? Think of any pause as a catalyst that will increase your faith.

Pray

Dear Lord, thank You for giving me strength when I feel my faith waiver.

Day 360

My suffering was good for me, for it taught me to pay attention to your decrees.

Psalm 119:71 (NLT)

Reflect

To live is to suffer, to survive is to find some meaning in the suffering.

Friedrich Nietzsche, philosopher

Act

When you experience hard times, use those difficulties to grow and become a better person.

Pray

Help me to infuse my life with Your healing power.

Day 361

Jesus replied, "Don't let anyone mislead you."

Mark 13:5 (NLT)

Reflect

Some of us think holding on makes us strong; but sometimes it is letting go.

Hermann Hesse, writer

Act

If you feel that someone twisted the truth or if something doesn't quite feel right in your heart, quiet your thoughts and feel Jesus's presence.

Pray

Father, I turn to You to help strengthen my discernment. Guide me on the right path.

Day 362

For they loved human praise more than praise from God.

John 12:43 (NIV)

Reflect

The best way to find yourself is to lose yourself in the service of others.

Mahatma Gandhi

Act

Focus on the One who truly matters by aligning your thoughts and actions with His will and your gifts.

Pray

Oh Heavenly Father, give me a heart like the heart of Jesus, so that I can serve others in Your name.

Day 363

For though the righteous fall seven times, they rise again, but the wicked stumble when calamity strikes.

Proverbs 24:16 (NIV)

Reflect

Experience is simply the name we give our mistakes.

Oscar Wilde, poet and playwright

Act

Let go of your fear of failure and focus on doing your best. Be proud of your wonderfully imperfect journey.

Pray

Heavenly Father, when I become stuck because I am afraid of trying something new, remind me that mistakes pave the way to success.

Day 364

So in Christ Jesus you are all children of God through faith.

Galatians 3:26 (NIV)

Reflect

Faith is deliberate confidence in the character of God whose ways you may not understand at the time.

Oswald Chambers, author and evangelist

Act

Be an ambassador of His love by freeing yourself from worry.

Pray

Heavenly Father, I am a messenger of Your Word.

Day 365

You said, "Listen now, and I will speak; I will question you, and you shall answer me."

Job 42:4 (NIV)

Reflect

Observe due measure, for right timing is in all things the most important factor.

Hesiod, poet

Act

Next time something difficult befalls you and you wonder why it happened, remember that God answers questions in His time and His way.

Pray

Father, help me find peace with all that is unanswered in my life.

Made in United States
Orlando, FL
06 November 2024